Aphrodite explores the many myths and meanings of the Greek goddess of love, sex and beauty. One of the most widely worshipped and popular deities in Greek antiquity, Aphrodite emerges from the imaginations of the ancient Greek writers and artists as a multifaceted, powerful and charismatic figure. This volume explores the importance of Aphrodite for the ancient Greeks, as well as her enduring influence as a symbol of beauty, adornment, love and sexuality in contemporary culture. In a wide-ranging investigation of the universality of Aphrodite's power and significance, this volume illuminates the numerous intricate levels of divinity embodied by the alluring figure of Aphrodite.

Aphrodite offers new insights into the ancient texts and artistic representations of the goddess, as well as a comprehensive survey of the current scholarship about the origins and interpretations of Aphrodite, whilst also highlighting her eternal popular appeal across cultures and generations. A goddess of love who is not afraid to enter the battlefield; a goddess of bodily adornment who is the first to appear totally nude; a goddess born of the sea who emerges into the open sky: Aphrodite is a polyvalent deity, plural in nature, function and significance.

Monica S. Cyrino is Professor of Classics at the University of New Mexico. Her research focuses on the intersection of the ancient world and popular culture. She is the author of *In Pandora's Jar: Lovesickness in Early Greek Poetry* (1995), and *Big Screen Rome* (2005).

Gods and Heroes of the Ancient World

Series editor Susan Deacy
Roehampton University

Routledge is pleased to present an exciting new series, Gods and Heroes of the Ancient World. These figures from antiquity are embedded in our culture, many functioning as the source of creative inspiration for poets, novelists, artists, composers and filmmakers. Concerned with their multifaceted aspects within the world of ancient paganism and how and why these figures continue to fascinate, the books provide a route into understanding Greek and Roman polytheism in the 21st century.

These concise and comprehensive guides provide a thorough understanding of each figure, offering the latest in critical research from the leading scholars in the field in an accessible and approachable form, making them ideal for undergraduates in Classics and related disciplines.

Each volume includes illustrations, time charts, family trees and maps where appropriate.

Also available:

Apollo
Fritz Graf

Prometheus
Carol Dougherty

Perseus
Daniel Ogden

Medea
Emma Griffiths

Athena
Susan Deacy

Dionysos
Richard Seaford

Zeus
Keith Dowden

Oedipus
Lowell Edmunds

Susan Deacy is Lecturer in Greek History and Literature at Roehampton University. Her main research interests are Greek religion, and gender and sexuality. Publications include the co-edited volumes *Rape in Antiquity* (1997), and *Athena in the Classical World* (2001), and the monograph *A Traitor to Her Sex? Athena the Trickster* (forthcoming).

APHRODITE

Monica S. Cyrino

Routledge
Taylor & Francis Group

LONDON AND NEW YORK

First published 2010
by Routledge
2 Park Square, Milton Park, Abingdon, Oxon OX14 4RN

Simultaneously published in the USA and Canada
by Routledge
270 Madison Avenue, New York, NY 10016

Routledge is an imprint of the Taylor & Francis Group, an informa business

Typeset in Utopia by
RefineCatch Limited, Bungay, Suffolk
Printed and bound in Great Britain by
CPI Antony Rowe, Chippenham, Wiltshire

British Library Cataloguing in Publication Data
A catalogue record for this book is available from the British Library

Library of Congress Cataloging in Publication Data
Cyrino, Monica Silveira.
Aphrodite / Monica S. Cyrino.
p. cm.
Includes index.
I. Title.
BL820.V5C97 2010
292.2′114–dc22
                    2009040543

ISBN10: 0–415–77522–1 (hbk)
ISBN10: 0–415–77523–X (pbk)

ISBN13: 978–0–415–77522–9 (hbk)
ISBN13: 978–0–415–77523–6 (pbk)

For Frances, Heidi and Alena
avatars of the goddess

CONTENTS

SERIES FOREWORD

It is proper for a person who is beginning any serious discourse and task to begin first with the gods.

(Demosthenes, *Epistula* 1.1)

WHY GODS AND HEROES?

The gods and heroes of classical antiquity are part of our culture. Many function as sources of creative inspiration for poets, novelists, artists, composers, filmmakers and designers. Greek tragedy's enduring appeal has ensured an ongoing familiarity with its protagonists' experiences and sufferings, while the choice of Minerva as the logo of one of the newest British universities, the University of Lincoln, demonstrates the ancient gods' continued emblematic potential. Even the world of management has used them as representatives of different styles: Zeus and the "club" culture for example, and Apollo and the "role" culture (see C. Handy, *The Gods of Management: Who they are, how they work and why they fail*, London, 1978).

This series is concerned with how and why these figures continue to fascinate and intrigue. But it has another aim too, namely to explore their strangeness. The familiarity of the gods and heroes risks obscuring a vital difference between modern meanings and ancient functions and purpose. With certain exceptions, people today do not worship them, yet to the Greeks and Romans they were real beings in a system comprising literally hundreds of divine powers. These range from the major gods, each of whom was worshipped in many guises via their epithets or "surnames," to the heroes – deceased individuals associated with local communities – to other figures such as daemons and nymphs. The landscape was dotted with sanctuaries, while natural features such as mountains, trees and rivers were thought to be inhabited by religious beings.

Studying ancient paganism involves finding strategies to comprehend a world where everything was, in the often quoted words of Thales, "full of gods."

In order to get to grips with this world, it is necessary to set aside our preconceptions of the divine, shaped as they are in large part by Christianised notions of a transcendent, omnipotent God who is morally good. The Greeks and Romans worshipped numerous beings, both male and female, who looked, behaved and suffered like humans, but who, as immortals, were not bound by the human condition. Far from being omnipotent, each had limited powers: even the sovereign, Zeus/Jupiter, shared control of the universe with his brothers Poseidon/Neptune (the sea) and Hades/Pluto (the underworld). Lacking a creed or anything like an organised church, ancient paganism was open to continual reinterpretation, with the result that we should not expect to find figures with a uniform essence. It is common to begin accounts of the pantheon with a list of the major gods and their function(s) (Hephaistos/Vulcan: craft, Aphrodite/Venus: love, and Artemis/Diana: the hunt and so on), but few are this straightforward. Aphrodite, for example, is much more than the goddess of love, vital though that function is. Her epithets include *hetaira* ("courtesan") and *porne* ("prostitute"), but also attest roles as varied as patron of the citizen body (*pandemos*: "of all the people") and protectress of seafaring (*Euploia, Pontia, Limenia*).

Recognising this diversity, the series consists not of biographies of each god or hero (though such have been attempted in the past), but of investigations into their multifaceted aspects within the complex world of ancient paganism. Its approach has been shaped partly in response to two distinctive patterns in previous research. Until the middle of the twentieth century, scholarship largely took the form of studies of individual gods and heroes. Many works presented a detailed appraisal of such issues as each figure's origins, myth and cult; these include L.R. Farnell's examination of major deities in his *Cults of the Greek States* (five volumes, Oxford, 1896–1909) and A.B. Cook's huge three-volume *Zeus* (Cambridge, 1914–1940). Others applied theoretical developments to the study of gods and heroes, notably (and in the closest existing works to a uniform series), K. Kerényi in his investigations of gods as Jungian archetypes, including *Prometheus: Archetypal image of human existence* (English trans. London, 1963) and *Dionysos: Archetypal image of indestructible life* (English trans. London, 1976).

In contrast, under the influence of French structuralism, the later part of the century saw a deliberate shift away from research into particular gods and heroes towards an investigation of the system of which they were part. Fuelled by a conviction that the study of isolated gods could not do justice to the dynamics of ancient religion, the pantheon came to be represented as a logical and coherent network in which the various powers were systematically opposed to one another. In a classic study by J.-P. Vernant, for example, the Greek concept of space was shown to be consecrated through the opposition between Hestia (goddess of the hearth – fixed space) and Hermes (messenger and traveller god – moveable space: Vernant, *Myth and Thought among the Greeks* London, 1983, 127–75). The gods as individual entities were far from neglected however, as may be exemplified by the works by Vernant, and his colleague M. Detienne, on particular deities, including Artemis, Dionysos and Apollo: see, most recently, Detienne's *Apollon, le couteau en main: une approche expérimentale du polythéisme grec* (Paris, 1998).

In a sense, this series is seeking a middle ground. While approaching its subjects as unique (if diverse) individuals, it pays attention to their significance as powers within the collectivity of religious beings. *Gods and Heroes of the Ancient World* sheds new light on many of the most important religious beings of classical antiquity; it also provides a route into understanding Greek and Roman polytheism in the twenty-first century.

The series is intended to interest the general reader as well as being geared to the needs of students in a wide range of fields from Greek and Roman religion and mythology, classical literature and anthropology, to Renaissance literature and cultural studies. Each book presents an authoritative, accessible and refreshing account of its subject via three main sections. The introduction brings out what it is about the god or hero that merits particular attention. This is followed by a central section which introduces key themes and ideas, including (to varying degrees) origins, myth, cult, and representations in literature and art. Recognising that the heritage of myth is a crucial factor in its continued appeal, the reception of each figure since antiquity forms the subject of the third part of the book. The books include illustrations of each god/hero and, where appropriate, time charts, family trees and maps. An annotated bibliography synthesises past research and indicates useful follow-up reading.

For convenience, the masculine terms "gods" and "heroes" have been selected for the series title, although (and with an apology for the male-dominated language) the choice partly reflects ancient usage in that the Greek *theos* ("god") is used of goddesses too. For convenience and consistency, Greek spellings are used for ancient names, except for famous Latinised exceptions, and bc/ad has been selected rather than bce/ce.

I am indebted to Catherine Bousfield, the editorial assistant until 2004, who (literally) dreamt up the series and whose thoroughness and motivation brought it close to its launch. The hard work and efficiency of her successor, Matthew Gibbons, has overseen its progress to publication, and the former classics publisher of Routledge, Richard Stoneman, has provided support and expertise throughout. The anonymous readers for each proposal gave frank and helpful advice, while the authors' commitments to advancing scholarship while producing accessible accounts of their designated subjects has made it a pleasure to work with them.

Susan Deacy, Roehampton University, June 2005

ACKNOWLEDGMENTS

It is with great appreciation that I acknowledge Peter Rohowsky at The Picture Desk in New York City for his superb professional assistance in securing permissions for the images that appear in this volume. Thanks to Dean Felipe Gonzales of the University of New Mexico, and to Pocket Venus Productions, for financial support towards the purchase of permissions fees.

I am very grateful to the series editor, Susan Deacy, for her encouragement at the outset of this venture; to Matthew Gibbons at Routledge for his patience and support; and to Lalle Pursglove at Routledge for her help throughout the production process.

Many sincere thanks go to Amy C. Smith and Sadie Pickup, who organized an extraordinary conference, Aphrodite Revealed, at the University of Reading in May 2008, and to the brilliant scholars, presenters and participants from all over the world who were the source of so many ideas and insights for this present endeavor, especially Graham Anderson, Lisa Brody, Kassandra Jackson, Vered Lev Kenaan, Thomas Kiely, Christine Kondoleon, Rachel Kousser, Sophie Montel, Elisabetta Pala, Chryssanthi Papadopoulou, Vinciane Pirenne-Delforge, Gabriella Pironti, Mary Plant and Anja Ulbrich. Thanks to you all for an exciting and, indeed, revealing experience.

I am profoundly indebted to my friend and fellow acolyte of the goddess, Stephanie Budin, for her generous and expert scholarly advice on all aspects of this project, her meticulous appraisal of the manuscript at every stage of its evolution, and her gracious good cheer whenever I needed a confidence boost.

My deepest thanks are also due to my colleague, Lorenzo F. Garcia, Jr., for his careful reading of and perceptive comments on the manuscript in progress, and to my friend and mentor, Jon Solomon, for his exceptional guidance on all things cinematic and Cyprian. Any infelicities of thought, judgment or expression left in this volume remain stubbornly mine.

Cheers also to my Classics students, especially Keith Alexander Woodell, Scott Barnard, Trigg Settle, Carl Young and Caley McGuill, who offered a constant supply of inspiration and support while I was working on this project.

Lastly, my heartfelt gratitude goes to my husband, the only one who really knows what it takes.

LIST OF ILLUSTRATIONS

WHY APHRODITE?

1

INTRODUCING APHRODITE

WHO IS APHRODITE?

Aphrodite is the ancient Greek goddess of erotic love and beauty. She is known to the Greeks by many names, traits and narratives. She is *aphrogenēs*, the "foam-born" goddess, born from the sea spume around the severed genitals of Ouranos, the primordial Heavens. She is *Dios thugatēr*, "daughter of Zeus," offspring of the Olympian sky god's union with the sea goddess Dione. Aphrodite's cultural heritage reveals Near Eastern, Indo-European and Cypriot features. She is invoked as *Cypris, Paphia, Cythereia* and *Ourania*. Love and sexuality are hers: *ta aphrodisia* are literally "the things that belong to Aphrodite." She is the goddess of *mixis*, the "mingling" of individual bodies in sexual, and sometimes military, fusion. She is the divine source of *peithō*, "persuasion," *eros*, "sexual desire," and *himeros*, "longing." Aphrodite is venerated as *Pandēmos*, "She who Belongs to all the People," and poets describe her as *Philommeidēs*, "smile loving." She is especially revered by prostitutes and seafarers. Aphrodite is the goddess of *kosmēsis*, "adornment," and she is intrinsically *chruseē*, "golden." Her attributes include jewelry, floral garlands, perfume and mirrors. The Graces and the Hours make up Aphrodite's principal immortal entourage. Among mortals, Aphrodite favors the Trojans, especially her lover, Anchises, and her son, Aeneas, as well as the celebrity couple, Helen and Paris. But Aphrodite can also be fierce when scorned, as in the case of Hippolytus. Aphrodite is the *Anadyomenē*, the goddess who "rises up from the sea," and her aquatic *anodos* is linked to her marine cult titles *Pontia* and *Pelagia*, "She of the Sea," *Euploia*, "She of the Smooth Sailing," and *Limenia*, "She of the Harbor." Aphrodite is worshipped in port towns and on mountain tops. Cockle shells, swans, geese, sparrows and doves are all sacred to her. Aphrodite's influence extends over the intermingled realms of sky, land and sea. Her extraordinary power still prevails in the world today.

Figure 1.1 Aphrodite of Arles. Roman copy after Praxiteles, *ca.* 350 BC. The Art Archive/Musée du Louvre Paris/Gianni Dagli Orti.

APHRODITE EMERGES

What does Aphrodite mean to the ancient Greeks? With what concepts is she associated? What does it mean to worship her? For the people of the ancient Greek-speaking world, Aphrodite is a goddess of immense authority and universal significance. One of the most widely worshipped deities in Greek antiquity, Aphrodite is venerated in many different religious cults all over the Mediterranean. Aphrodite also emerges in several important ways in the daily lives of the ancient Greeks: how they conduct their erotic relationships; how they seek to enhance their physical appearance; and how they travel on the all-surrounding sea. Aphrodite enjoys a broad geographic sphere of influence across the ancient civilized world, from the island of Cyprus in the east to the island of Sicily in the west, and she was especially honored in the harbors of the great cities, such as Athens, Naukratis and Syracuse. A goddess of love who is not afraid to enter the battlefield; a goddess of bodily adornment who is the first to appear totally nude; a goddess born of the sea who emerges into the open sky: Aphrodite is a polyvalent deity, plural in nature and meaning, but never fragmented.

The following points arise out of the ancient sources as the three most important ideas for understanding the Greek conception of Aphrodite. These ideas will appear again and again in the subsequent chapters that investigate the myths, images and discourses about Aphrodite.

- *Anodos* or "going up." Aphrodite is the goddess who emerges from the sea into the sky, who is revealed in all her immortal beauty and radiance, whose divinity is unmistakable even under a cunning disguise. The idea of Aphrodite's epiphany, especially the immediacy of her stunning appearance, is central to her meaning and power. She is the *Anadyomenē*, from the Greek verb *anaduomai*, "to rise up," the goddess who rises up before our astonished eyes.
- *Kosmēsis* or "adornment." Aphrodite's lovely appearance and potent physicality are fundamental to understanding her immortal function and significance. In the ancient Greek sources, the epiphany of the goddess is accompanied by intricate and detailed depictions of her golden jewelry, brilliant clothing, floral garlands, and the fragrance of perfume and incense. Such physical adornment enhances Aphrodite's sway over the realms of erotic attraction and allure.
- *Mixis* or "mingling." Aphrodite is the goddess of *mixis*, the blending of bodies in intimate physical contact, both sexual and martial. As the divine embodiment of *mixis*, Aphrodite also represents the union of sea, land and sky, as she expresses her capacity for mediation within those elemental networks. Wherever these realms touch and mingle, wherever the boundaries are blurred in between them, that is where you will find Aphrodite.

THE EVIDENCE FOR APHRODITE

How do we set about discovering the nature of Aphrodite? What evidence can we find in ancient Greek mythology, literary sources, artistic representations, cults and festivals? While Aphrodite was certainly an object of devout cultic veneration in antiquity, our conception of her is influenced by her iconographical representation in myth, literature and art. Aphrodite emerges out of the imaginations of the ancient Greek artists and writers, and her distinctively polyvalent identity as a goddess becomes manifest in numerous myths and images as portrayed in diverse genres of literature and art. Indeed, it is quite likely the ancient Greek poets and artists combined aspects of mythology and cult in creating their depictions of Aphrodite.

As we explore the depictions, activities and meanings of Aphrodite, we will look to the earliest Greek literary sources dating from the eighth, seventh and sixth centuries BC. This will include primarily the Homeric epic poems, the *Iliad* and the *Odyssey*; the *Homeric Hymns*, especially the fifth and sixth Homeric hymns, which are addressed to Aphrodite; the summaries of the lost epic poem, the *Cypria*, a work from the early epic cycle; the mythological writings of Hesiod, especially the *Theogony*; and the erotic verses of the archaic lyric poets, such as Sappho, Mimnermus and Ibycus. In addition, we will consider the representation of Aphrodite in some fifth-century BC works, especially the *Hippolytus*, a tragedy by the Athenian dramatist Euripides (produced in 428 BC); as well as *The Histories* recorded by the Greek historian Herodotus (*ca.* 484–425 BC). Among the Hellenistic literary texts, we will examine Aphrodite's appearance in the epic poem the *Argonautica* by Apollonius of Rhodes (third century BC), and also several epigrams and other verses by Hellenistic poets of the third century BC and after. When we consult sources from later antiquity, such as the travel writings of Pausanias (second century AD), it is because these later authors illuminate some aspect of Aphrodite's persona as depicted in the earlier texts. In looking for artistic representations of Aphrodite, we will consider both small- and large-scale depictions of the goddess that were produced throughout Greek antiquity, from fifth-century vase painting and small terracotta figurines, to life-size marble statues of the later Hellenistic period. Although no one text or image can encompass the full polyvalence of Aphrodite, each of these sources will offer crucial information about how the ancient Greeks viewed her myths, meanings and functions.

OVERVIEW

In the following chapters, we will investigate several key themes that exemplify and define the idea of Aphrodite. First we will consider Aphrodite's beginnings, both the ancient mythological narratives of her birth, as well as the modern scholarly theories about her geographic and cultural origins. Next we will explore the meaning of Aphrodite as the goddess of *mixis* whose divine authority permeates the interrelated realms of love, sex and warfare. The following chapter examines Aphrodite's welcome influence over the process of beautification for erotic allure, as we also look at how the goddess herself is physically depicted, both fully adorned and naked. Next comes a survey of Aphrodite's relationships with various mortals, highlighting how each interaction represents some significant aspect of her divinity. After that we will contemplate Aphrodite's nature as a goddess who emerges from the sea into the sky, and thus shares in the attributes of both realms. And finally, we will reflect upon Aphrodite's enduring power as a symbol of love and beauty in contemporary popular culture.

In Euripides' play the *Alcestis* (produced in 438 BC), which explores the complex impulses inherent in conjugal love, the Greek hero Herakles arrives to save the day by reuniting his grieving host, Admetus, with his recently deceased wife, Alcestis. When the hero first appears onstage more than halfway through the play – inebriated, boisterous, a little dense, but ever magnanimous – he does not completely understand the dangerous ambiguities of the day's events; nevertheless he delivers a rousing "*carpe diem*" speech to the grim-faced servants in the household of his host. Herakles enjoins them to stop worrying about their elusive mortality, bidding them worship the one deity who can make their brief and unpredictable lives happy now.

> Enjoy yourself! The life you live today
> is yours, and all the rest belongs to fortune.
> Honor the god who is by far the sweetest
> to mortals: honor kindly Aphrodite.
> As for all the rest, forget it. Listen
> to what I say, if you think it makes sense.
>
> (*Alcestis* 700–93, trans. Svarlien, 2007)

KEY THEMES

2

BIRTH, ORIGINS, NAMES

In this chapter, we will explore Aphrodite's beginnings, starting with the question of Aphrodite's birth as a divine figure in Greek mythology. First, we will consider the distinctive mythic variants in the earliest literary accounts of her birth and delve into how these fundamental stories might reflect the essential aspects of her manifold divinity. Next we will examine the possible geographical, chronological, ethnic and cultural origins of Aphrodite, while acknowledging the controversies and challenges we face in attempting to settle upon a single source or derivation for this cosmopolitan goddess. Lastly we will discuss some of the most popular names and significant epithets of the goddess and investigate their possible associations with her myths, appearances in Greek literature and cultic origins.

BIRTH

Aphrodite's earliest birth stories in Greek myth explicitly illuminate her multifaceted nature and describe her many evolving characteristics in the mythology, literature and cults of ancient Greece. These original Greek literary myths portray Aphrodite as having two distinct ancestral pedigrees, while both accounts make clear that the ancient Greeks associated Aphrodite with the realms of the sky and sea. In one early account, Aphrodite is shown to be born directly from the maimed body of Ouranos, the primordial Greek god of the sky and the most basic personification of the heavens. When his severed genitals are thrown into the sea, Aphrodite arises out of the foamy waters into the bright air, thereby linking the aquatic and celestial domains. In another version, Aphrodite is depicted as the daughter of Zeus, the Olympian sky god and king of gods and mortals, and his consort, the goddess Dione. Although these literary myths differ in their narrative contours and plot details, both stories clearly imply Aphrodite's close relationship to the elemental principles of the sky and sea, her intimate association with the celestial masculine ideal, and her conspicuous presence at the highest pinnacles of divine power.

The castration of Ouranos

One of the earliest literary accounts of Aphrodite's birth and lineage comes to light in the *Theogony* of Hesiod, a lengthy mythological poem about the origins of the Greek gods and the genesis of the divine order, composed sometime in the eighth or seventh century BC. In Hesiod's

Figure 2.1 *The Birth of Venus*, detail. Sandro Botticelli, *ca.* 1485. The Art Archive/ Galleria degli Uffizi Florence/Alfredo Dagli Orti.

narrative version (*Theogony* 188–206), the birth of Aphrodite follows the brutal castration of the primordial sky god Ouranos, by his youngest Titan son, the wily Cronos. According to Hesiod, after Cronos committed this act of filial violence to attain supreme rule of the world, he threw his father's severed genitals into the sea, where the divine semen together with the salty sea spume mingled to form the *leukos aphros*, or "white foam" (190–91), and the goddess Aphrodite emerged from this auspicious mixture.

> The genitalia themselves, freshly cut with flint, were thrown
> Clear of the mainland into the restless, white-capped sea,
> Where they floated a long time. A white foam from the god-flesh
> Collected around them, and in that foam a maiden developed
> And grew. Her first approach to land was near holy Kythera
> And from there she floated on to the island of Kypros.
> There she came ashore, an awesome, beautiful divinity.
> Tender grass sprouted up under her slender feet.

> Aphrodite
> Is her name in speech human and divine, since it was in foam
> She was nourished. But she is also called Kythereia since
> She reached Kythera, and Kyprogenes because she was born
> On the surf-line of Kypros, and Philommedes because she loves
> The organs of sex, from which she made her epiphany.
> Eros became her companion, and ravishing Desire waited on her
> At her birth and when she made her debut among the Immortals.
> From that moment on, among both gods and humans,
> She has fulfilled the honored function that includes
> Virginal sweet-talk, lovers' smiles and deceits
> And all of the gentle pleasures of sex.

(*Theogony* 188–206, trans. Lombardo, 1993)

Hesiod's exquisite narrative emphasizes several key elements intrinsic to the Greek conception of Aphrodite's divine nature. First, the birth of the goddess from the castrated genitals of Ouranos is a striking allegory for how the ancient Greek poets viewed the antagonistic nature of human sexuality, as the story signifies the goddess' intimate link to the violence, intensity and aggression that is inherent in the Greek notion of the erotic experience. The Hesiodic birth story also vividly underscores Aphrodite's direct origin from the sky god Ouranos, the supreme divinity in this primeval tale, while at the same time it demonstrates her close association to the transfer of divine power indicated in the foundational succession myth immediately preceding it. Hesiod's Aphrodite is thereby considered part of the earliest echelon of primordial Greek deities. Consistent with the ancient Greek belief that Aphrodite had aquatic associations, the goddess' profound connection to the realm of the sea is indicated by her initial emergence out of the foamy waves into the bright air. Moreover, woven into this birth narrative are numerous poetic components that create the ambience of a genuine Greek cultic hymn. For example, Hesiod mentions Aphrodite's favorite cult places, the islands of Cythera and Cyprus (192–93); he cites and describes the origins of her traditional cult epithets, *Cythereia* (198), *Cyprogenēs* (199), and *Philommēdēs* (200); he also lists a few of her divine companions, including Eros, personification of lust, and Himeros, personification of desire (201); and finally, he cleverly elucidates the folk etymology of Aphrodite's name through this story of her maritime nativity – Aphrodite is the goddess born from the *aphros*, or "sea foam" (195–98). In Hesiod's foundational birth story, the primordial goddess Aphrodite is shown to be the glorious mistress of all she touches, casting her powerful divine influence of refinement, beauty and harmony over a wide array of settings: from the smoothing of the seas and the generation of supple grass beneath her feet, to the whispered flirtations and sweet lies told by lovers everywhere.

Daughter of Zeus and Dione

Another early literary explanation of Aphrodite's parentage is given in the grand epic poems of Homer, the *Iliad* and the *Odyssey*, which were composed sometime in the eighth or seventh century BC. In Homer's account, several times Aphrodite is called *Dios thugatēr*, or "daughter of Zeus," the great Olympian god of the sky who is the chief of all gods and mortals, while her mother is introduced once as the goddess Dione (also told in Apollodorus, *The Library* 1.3.1). Although there is a good deal of uncertainty about Dione's identity, etymologically her name appears to be a feminine form cognate to the oblique forms of the name Zeus (*Dios*, *Dion* etc.), which may indicate there is some common mythological antecedent or even assimilation between the two figures as a divine celestial couple. Dione shared a cult with Zeus at Dodona in northwestern Greece, so in linguistic terms Dione may indeed be a sky goddess. Yet Hesiod tells us in his narrative poem that Dione is a type of sea goddess, specifically an Oceanid, one of the daughters of the Titans, Oceanos and Tethys (*Theogony* 353): so the earliest Greek literary account places Dione securely within the older stratum of Greek gods and links her to the primordial deities of the deep waters. Through her Homeric "parents," then, Aphrodite is again linked to the sea and the sky. In her one appearance in the Homeric epic (in *Iliad* book 5), Dione has a prominent role as the provider of maternal affection to soothe her "daughter," Aphrodite, who is thereby represented as firmly ensconced within the Olympian family hierarchy as a goddess of a later generation.

Aphrodite has two major appearances within the decidedly martial milieu of the *Iliad*. In both scenes the goddess attempts to save a mortal she loves from the dangers of the battlefield by enfolding him in her concealing embrace, and in both of these instances the epic refers to her as *Dios thugatēr*, "daughter of Zeus." In book 3 of the *Iliad*, Aphrodite intervenes during the *monomachia*, the hand-to-hand combat between the two men who are fighting over Helen, the beautiful mortal queen beloved by the goddess: Paris, Prince of Troy, Aphrodite's favorite and the lover of Helen, and Menelaus, King of Sparta and Helen's legal husband. In Homer's account, Menelaus knocks Paris down and is dragging him from the field by the crest of his helmet, when the goddess, here named "Aphrodite, daughter of Zeus" (3.374), rushes in and unsnaps Paris' chinstrap, freeing him from the Spartan's grasp.

> But Aphrodite, Zeus' daughter, had all this
> In sharp focus and snapped the oxhide chinstrap,
> Leaving Menelaus clenching an empty helmet,
> Which the hero, spinning like a discus thrower,
> Heaved into the hands of the Greek spectators.
> Then he went back for the kill.
>   But Aphrodite
> Whisked Paris away with the sleight of a goddess,
> Enveloping him in mist, and lofted him into
> The incensed air of his vaulted bedroom.
>
> (*Iliad* 3.374–82, trans. Lombardo, 1997)

At this point in the narrative of book 3, Aphrodite takes Paris safely back to his chamber in the Trojan palace, and the goddess urges a reluctant Helen to join him in bed. It is interesting to note that Helen's direct paternity from the god Zeus is also referred to twice in this passage (3,418, 426), since Helen is considered by some scholars to be a Spartan avatar of Aphrodite: at least Helen possesses an unquestionable privilege as one of the goddess' most favored mortals in Greek mythology. In a later literary source, the *Helen* (dated 412 BC), a play by the Athenian dramatist Euripides (*ca.* 480–406 BC), the title character uses a rather sisterly tone as she addresses Aphrodite as "daughter of Dione," *korē Diōnēs* (*Helen* 1098).

Aphrodite's next appearance in the *Iliad* comes during the fighting mayhem of book 5, where the goddess, named *Dios thugatēr*, "daughter of Zeus" (5.312), again hurries to the battlefield to save a vulnerable person: this time, it is the Trojan warrior, Aeneas, her son by the mortal, Anchises. Under heavy assault by advancing Greeks, Aeneas has been wounded – his hip socket gravely smashed by a boulder flung by the Greek hero, Diomedes – and the Trojan sinks to the ground.

> That would have been the end of Aeneas,
> But his mother, Aphrodite, Zeus' daughter,
> Who bore Aeneas to Anchises the oxherd,
> Had all this in sharp focus. Her milk-white arms
> Circled around him and she enfolded him
> In her radiant robe to prevent the Greeks
> From killing him with a spear to the chest.
>
> (*Iliad* 5.311–17, trans. Lombardo, 1997)

But as she is carrying her son from the field, Aphrodite herself is wounded by Diomedes, who thrusts his spear into her wrist, stabbing her through the folds of her dress. Diomedes adds insult to injury, as he cruelly taunts the goddess, here again called *Dios thugatēr*, "daughter of Zeus" (5.348), for being unwarlike and threatens to do her even worse harm.

> "Get out of the war, daughter of Zeus!
> Don't you have enough to do distracting
> Weak women? Keep meddling in war and
> You'll learn to shiver when it's even mentioned."
>
> (*Iliad* 5.348–51, trans. Lombardo, 1997)

With her wrist pierced and bleeding, Aphrodite shrieks and drops Aeneas, who is saved by the god, Apollo; stricken with pain, she is helped off the battlefield by Iris, as they borrow the chariot of Ares, god of war, to fly back up to Olympus. There Aphrodite finds Dione, *mētros heēs*, "her mother," and falls into her lap (5.370–71). Dione expresses great maternal concern and soft-hearted tenderness towards Aphrodite, as Homer tells us, by "cradling her daughter in her arms, and stroking her with her hand" (5.371–72), calling her *philon tekos*, "my poor baby" (5.373) and *teknon emon*, "my child" (5.382). Later, the god Zeus appears on the scene and verbally confirms his own parental relationship with Aphrodite, calling her *teknon emon*, "my child" (5.428), when he reminds her that warfare is not her area of expertise.

Aphrodite also makes a memorable appearance in book 8 of the *Odyssey*, in the song of the bard Demodocus, who entertains Odysseus during his visit to the Phaeacians. In Demodocus' narrative (8.266–369), Aphrodite is represented as being firmly part of the Olympian family hierarchy, and twice she is referred to as *Dios thugatēr*, "daughter of Zeus" (8.308, 320), while the racy anecdote also suggests that she is clearly subordinate to his paternal control. As Demodocus tells it, Hephaestus, the blacksmith god, discovers his wife, Aphrodite, is having an affair with Ares, the handsome god of war. So the craftsman god devises a trap to ensnare the adulterous pair in fine but unbreakable chains. Hephaestus calls out to all the gods to witness his wife's scandalous behavior, naming the one who scorns him "Aphrodite, daughter of Zeus" (8.308). As the cheaters remain on display for the jeers and wisecracks of the assembled male gods, Hephaestus demands repayment of his dowry investment from Zeus, Aphrodite's father.

> "But they're staying put in my little snare
> Until her father returns all of the gifts
> I gave him to marry this bitch-faced girl,
> His beautiful, yes, but faithless daughter."
>
> (*Odyssey* 8.317–20, trans. Lombardo, 2000)

Like the two *Iliad* passages, the *Odyssey* episode clearly asserts Aphrodite's place within the Olympian family structure as the daughter of Zeus. But the *Odyssey* passage makes her filial position even more emphatic by representing the goddess in the midst of a grim family drama, as the daughter of a *paterfamilias* who is now compelled to pay reparations to his son-in-law for her adulterous behavior.

All three of the Homeric epic passages naming Aphrodite as *Dios thugatēr*, "daughter of Zeus," highlight key elements of the goddess' divine nature as imagined by the ancient Greeks. By linking her to Zeus, the Olympian sky god, Aphrodite's association with the sky and the principal source of divine power in the classical Greek pantheon are both emphasized. In casting the sky-named sea goddess Dione in the role of Aphrodite's mother, the Greek epic poems suggest Aphrodite's kinship with the sea or sky, or perhaps both simultaneously. Moreover, these epic passages also demonstrate Aphrodite's intimacy with the martial realm of warfare, both in intervening to save her mortal favorites (not always successfully) from the perils of the battlefield, and in enjoying an erotic tryst (not completely trouble-free) with Ares, god of war, her favorite immortal lover. In a later discussion, we will see how the concept of warfare in the ancient Greek representation of Aphrodite interacts closely with her divine dimensions of love and sexuality, and is to some extent also intermingled in the goddess' familiar relationships with mortals.

ORIGINS

Let us now turn to the question of Aphrodite's "real" origins as the classical Greek deity of love and sexuality and a figure of divine worship for the ancient Greeks. There is no doubt the Greek goddess Aphrodite belonged to the Greek pantheon of gods and was a fully functional cast member in the tales of Greek mythology by the late eighth or early seventh century BC, as attested by her noteworthy appearances in the poems of Homer and Hesiod that describe her mythological birth, parentage and other activities. What is not clear, however, is whether Aphrodite developed as an indigenous Hellenic goddess on Greek soil (and, if so, when), or whether, she emigrated to Greece from outside the Greek-speaking world sometime before or during the eighth century BC, that is, before the works of Homer and Hesiod were composed. Or perhaps there was an early native Hellenic proto-Aphrodite evolving along just fine by herself sometime before the eighth century BC, who then encountered and was influenced by the various foreign characteristics of an imported goddess or goddesses, after which these several divine elements mingled and merged together to form the classical Greek Aphrodite. When considering the nature of such a multifaceted and complex goddess, the possible scenarios of her origin, diffusion and development are endless.

As is the case with many other gods in the Greek pantheon, there are ongoing, and sometimes quite vigorous, scholarly controversies over the specific geographical, ethnic, chronological and cultic origins of the goddess Aphrodite (most recently, with overview of scholarly controversies: Budin 2003). The argument over her origins has been raging for more than a hundred years, and it seems unlikely to diminish any time soon. Indeed, whatever "side" one takes in the origins debate, it can be said with certainty that the goddess Aphrodite was born into a very cosmopolitan Mediterranean world, a multicultural, multi-ethnic, multilingual environment of intense and lively international exchange in which ideas, images, texts, goods and even religious cults were traded quickly and easily across the borders of sea and land. Wherever Aphrodite came from, whenever that happened, and wherever (and whenever) she turned up, the thorny question necessarily arises about the actual process of cultic transmission and any proposed or assumed religious syncretism that followed. How did the one Aphrodite – earlier, ostensibly more

Eastern, or more martial, for example – become the other Aphrodite – later, maybe more Greek, or less warlike, but still fierce? It is difficult to formulate, much less answer, such an elaborate and obstacle-prone question with anything approaching comprehensiveness or precision. The controversy over Aphrodite's origins, therefore, given the complexities of the questions that scholars must ask and the ultimate elusiveness of the answers we seek, may simply be impossible to solve. But let us sort through the alternatives among the three basic theories concerning Aphrodite's possible origins and her subsequent introduction into the Greek pantheon of gods.

Near Eastern Aphrodite

Many modern scholars, following a school of thought that dates back at least to the nineteenth century, believe Aphrodite is not of Hellenic origin at all, but like some other deities in the Greek pantheon, as they claim, she was introduced into Greece from the Near East (most recently, with review of relevant scholarship: Breitenberger 2007). These scholars cite as supporting evidence for this principally "orientalist" hypothesis the pervasive influence of Near Eastern culture on Greek art, literature, and mythology generally during the span of the eighth and seventh centuries BC, as the late Dark Age period (1100–800 BC) blossomed into the Archaic period in Greece. In addition, these scholars note the fact that there is no trace of Aphrodite's name or epithets in the record of the late Bronze Age Aegean civilization (ca. 1300–1100 BC); specifically, they point out that her name occurs nowhere on the Mycenaean Greek Linear B tablets, while the names of the majority of the Greek deities worshipped in the following centuries, such as Zeus, Hera, Hermes, Artemis and Athena, do appear in these documents. Therefore, this school of thought maintains that Aphrodite was most likely imported from Asia sometime before the eighth century BC, during the tumultuous and transitional interlude of cross-cultural exchange between the Near East and the Greek world, and that she probably arrived by way of the eastern and southern Aegean islands, and in particular via the island of Cyprus (see following section). Even after her adoption into the Greek pantheon around the eighth or seventh century BC, according to the advocates of the Near Eastern theory, the Greek texts and material artifacts from the Archaic and Classical periods indicate that Aphrodite retained a vestigial "oriental" quality in her mythology, cult, artistic iconography and literary appearances.

Some ancient Greek authors support the theory that the goddess Aphrodite came from the Near East, including the Greek historian Herodotus, who claims Aphrodite is Phoenician in origin. Herodotus reports in *The Histories* that the oldest sanctuary to the goddess called "Aphrodite *Ourania*" or "Heavenly" (1.105.2) was at Ascalon in Syria, a Phoenician settlement, and adds that it was also the Phoenicians who first brought her cult to the islands of Cyprus and Cythera.

> This temple [at Ascalon], as I find by inquiry, is the most ancient of all the temples dedicated to this goddess; for that in Cyprus was built after this, as the Cyprians themselves confess; and that in Cythera was erected by Phoenicians who came from the same part of Syria.
>
> (*The Histories* 1.105.2–3, trans. Cary, 1992)

But the core of the "orientalist" hypothesis rests on the perceived parallels and mutual associations between the eventual Greek Aphrodite and the Near Eastern goddesses of love and sexuality in their cultic, literary and artistic representations. A number of modern scholars believe that Aphrodite is in essence simply a Hellenized version of Ishtar or Inanna, the influential Near Eastern love-goddess figures, who, they contend, traveled east to west before she was adopted by the Greeks as Aphrodite, their own deity of love. In making their case, these scholars enumerate Aphrodite's many similarities, especially in her aggressive sexual attributes, to the Mesopotamian goddess Ishtar, who appears in the great Babylonian epic of Gilgamesh, or to her Sumerian counterpart, the goddess Inanna. They also argue there are numerous correspondences in cult and iconography between Aphrodite and Astarte, the Phoenician goddess of sexuality and warfare, such as the presence of doves and incense in her religious rituals, and the shared cult title "Queen of Heaven," which they claim is comparable to Aphrodite's epithet *Ourania*, "Heavenly." While Aphrodite is never called "Queen of Heaven" exactly, these scholars claim the correlation in epithets is textually supported by the testimony of Herodotus regarding the Phoenician origins of Aphrodite *Ourania*, or the "Heavenly" goddess. Moreover, some literary scholars suggest that stories and myths about Aphrodite recounted in the works of the Greek poets provide evidence of literary borrowing from the Near East (recently: West 1997). For example, they claim that some elements of the tale of Aphrodite and her lover, Anchises, as told in the *Homeric Hymn to Aphrodite* (hymn 5), parallel some aspects of Gilgamesh's refusal of Ishtar's sexual advances in the earlier epic. After examining the compositional structure of the myths and thematic motifs used by the poets Homer and Hesiod to depict Aphrodite, these scholars come to the conclusion that such narrative patterns may have been originally inspired by oriental models and thus strongly imply a Near Eastern origin for the goddess Aphrodite.

So if we accept this theory, the question still remains: just how did this east–west dissemination work? That is, how did Aphrodite eventually become Hellenized? The proponents of the "orientalist" hypothesis explain that the Near Eastern love-goddess figure was originally transported by travelers and traders to the southern and eastern Greek islands of the Aegean, chiefly to Cyprus, where the Greeks most likely were first exposed to her cult. Then, at some point during the transmission, the goddess was given a typically Greek varnish which would serve to distinguish her from her Near Eastern predecessors or prototypes. Thus, they argue, the Olympian Aphrodite is ultimately a composite figure, whose Greek character becomes more emphasized and markedly Hellenized as she is portrayed in Greek myth, poetry and art. Yet this school of thought also maintains that her Near Eastern origins continue to be reflected in the "oriental" flavor of the cultic, mythological and artistic portrayals of the goddess Aphrodite.

Cypriot Aphrodite

In the cult and worship of Aphrodite, the significance of the island of Cyprus, with its prominent cult sanctuary to the goddess at Paphos in the southwest corner of the island, as well as her other cult sites on the island, such as Amathus and Golgoi, is recognized by ancient authors and modern scholars alike. Indeed, there is broad scholarly consensus that Cyprus may have been the earliest cult place for the worship of Aphrodite by the Greeks (most recently, with extensive surveying of archaeological evidence and research: Ulbrich 2008; Karageorghis 2005; Pirenne-Delforge 1994). Moreover, many scholars agree that Cyprus may have also played a key role in the development of the eventual Greek goddess of love, and that the island may have somehow mediated Aphrodite's subsequent entry to the Greek mainland. Thus, as we will see below, the Cypriot hypothesis is not entirely incompatible with the Near Eastern theory of origin discussed above.

The traditional setting of Aphrodite's major cult sanctuary at Paphos on the island of Cyprus is deeply integrated into her earliest literary myths. The early Greek poets Homer and Hesiod both highlight the importance of Cyprus as the special place where the goddess feels most at home. In Hesiod's birth story, as we have seen earlier, Aphrodite approaches the island of Cythera before heading directly east to Cyprus, where she first comes ashore and her feet touch solid land (*Theogony*

192–95). In the *Odyssey*, the bard Demodocus ends his song with a detailed description of her sanctuary at Cyprus: after the discovery of her dalliance with Ares, Aphrodite goes home to Paphos to be washed and anointed by her attendants, the *Charites*, or Graces.

> The two of them, free at last from their crimp,
> Shot out of there, Ares to Thrace,
> And Aphrodite, who loves laughter and smiles,
> To Paphos on Cyprus, and her precinct there
> With its smoking altar. There the Graces
> Bathed her and rubbed her with ambrosial oil
> That glistens on the skin of the immortal gods.
> And then they dressed her in beautiful clothes,
> A wonder to see.
>
> (*Odyssey* 8.360–66, trans. Lombardo, 2000)

In the *Homeric Hymn to Aphrodite*, Aphrodite is called *Cypris*, "the Cyprian" (hymn 5.2), and in this poem, too, her spa-temple is located at Paphos on the island of Cyprus. There the Graces prepare her for her seduction of the Trojan oxherd, Anchises.

> The Cyprian shrine at Paphos, full of incense,
> Features her holy ground and fragrant altar.
> She went there, went inside, and shut the bright doors.
> And there the Graces bathed her and rubbed on her
> A holy oil that blooms on the undying –
> She kept this heavenly sweet perfume handy.
> Now dressed in every kind of gorgeous garment
> And gold-festooned, fun-loving Aphrodite
> Left fragrant Cyprus – straight to Troy she headed.
>
> (hymn 5.58–66, trans. Ruden, 2005)

So the ancient poets were keenly aware of the status of Cyprus as Aphrodite's favorite place, and her affinity for her sanctuary at Paphos is indisputable. But how exactly did the goddess come to be associated with the island? Some proponents of Aphrodite's "oriental" origins argue that the cult worship of Aphrodite at Paphos on Cyprus was established by the Phoenicians, who settled on the island sometime around the first millennium BC. The Phoenicians have long enjoyed a conventional role in Greek literature as seafaring traders and cultural intermediaries between east and west: as we have noted, Herodotus says the Phoenicians worshipped Aphrodite at Ascalon in Syria, and took this cult to Cyprus when they settled there (*The Histories* 1.105.2). Some scholars suggest that a few early-arriving Phoenicians may have been instrumental in either the building or refurbishing of Aphrodite's famous temple at Paphos, which apparently dates back to Mycenaean times (*ca.* 1200 BC); they also cite archaeological findings at other Aphrodite sanctuaries on the island as evidence of possible Phoenician influence as well (most recently, with review of scholarship: Breitenberger 2007). Consequently, they make the case that Phoenician traders and later settlers played a key role as mediators of the cult of Aphrodite, bringing her from the east to Greece, and thereby facilitating her eventual evolution into the Olympian goddess of love. So we would consider Cyprus to be a sort of ancient Mediterranean "Ellis Island" where the Near Eastern immigrant Aphrodite waited to be admitted onto the Greek mainland, so that she could be fully "naturalized" as a Hellenic deity.

Other scholars see the island of Cyprus as still more significant and even central to the evolution of the Greek goddess of love (most recently, with thorough explication of evidence: Ulbrich 2008; Karageorghis 2005; Budin 2003). Some scholars argue for the existence of an early native Cypriot proto-Aphrodite, significantly pre-dating the arrival of the Phoenicians in the ninth century BC, who was worshipped especially at Paphos during the late Mycenaean era and perhaps even earlier in the late Bronze Age (*ca.* 1300–1100 BC). This indigenous island goddess then developed into the fully realized Greek Aphrodite through the turbulent period of change during and following the Dark Ages (1100–800 BC). While some scholars accept the premise of an indigenous Cypriot goddess, they also suggest she may have been influenced early on by contacts with the Near East, both the Levant and further east to Mesopotamia: specifically, they claim she may have been influenced by the Near Eastern love-goddess types as they passed through the island with travelers and traders. Thus, it was this multilayered goddess figure, a native Cypriot with "oriental" accents, who was later transmitted to the mainland, where she became the classical Aphrodite represented in Greek mythology, art and literature.

Indo-European Aphrodite

A small but influential group of scholars advocate a predominantly Indo-European origin for the classical Greek Aphrodite (chiefly: Boedeker 1974; Friedrich 1978; Nagy 1990). Among all the origin theories and debates, the proponents of the Indo-European school of thought argue for the earliest appearance of Aphrodite on Hellenic soil, claiming that an Indo-European Aphrodite ancestor was brought to the Aegean area by the first speakers of Greek, perhaps as early as the middle Bronze Age (*ca.* 2000–1500 BC). These scholars suggest that Aphrodite initially arose from an Indo-European dawn goddess, who was one of the original divine members of the commonly shared Indo-European pantheon that also prominently featured a sky-father figure, *Dyēus*, the Indo-European precursor of the Greek sky god, Zeus. Through a primarily philological analysis, these scholars maintain that Aphrodite's nearest equivalent in extant ancient literature would be Ushas, the dawn goddess celebrated in the *Rig Veda*, a sacred collection of ancient Sanskrit hymns dedicated to the Hindu gods. According to this theory, after the first Greek speakers inherited the common Indo-European pantheon, at some point in prehistory the early Greek dawn-goddess figure split into two separate but related deities: Eos, the Greek goddess of the dawn, and Aphrodite.

This identification is chiefly supported by a series of literary and linguistic parallels posited between the Greek goddesses Aphrodite and Eos – originally one deity, as they claim – and their Indo-European cognate, Ushas, the Vedic dawn goddess. Ushas is celebrated in approximately twenty-one hymns of the *Rig Veda*, both praising her for her radiant beauty and sensuousness, and appealing to her to provide material wealth and riches. Advocates of the Indo-European theory call attention to several textual similarities described in the ancient mythological texts between the attributes, epithets and narrative functions of the Indic Ushas and those of the Greek Eos–Aphrodite. Such parallels include the goddesses' erotic beauty and aggressive sexuality; their shared association with the colors red, white and gold in their attributes; their links to celestial (solar and astral) figures; their relationships with mortal lovers and sons; and their emergence from the sea into the sky. Although the Greek writers never explicitly equate Aphrodite with a dawn goddess, her rising from the sea is strikingly described by Hesiod, as we have seen, in his version of Aphrodite's birth (*Theogony* 188–93), as well as by the poet of the shorter *Homeric Hymn to Aphrodite* (hymn 6).

I'll sing of gold-crowned, lovely Aphrodite,
Honored owner of Cyprian battlements
Set in the sea, where the wet-gushing west wind
And the soft-foaming, racketing waves bestowed her.

(hymn 6.1–5, trans. Ruden, 2005)

But the key element of the Indo-European argument is based on Aphrodite's close kinship in the ancient texts to the Greek sky god, whether her paternity is derived from Ouranos, the primordial element of the sky, as in Hesiod's birth story, or from Zeus, the Olympian sky god, as in the Homeric epics: both sky gods are attested as Aphrodite's "fathers" in the principal Greek versions of her birth myths. Similarly, in the Vedic tradition, Ushas is said to be "sky born," *divo-jā* (*Rig Veda* 6.65.1), and she is frequently called the daughter of the Indic sky father *Dyáus Pitar*. Moreover, they argue, just as Ushas is typically described by the formulaic epithet *diva(s) duhitár-*, "daughter of the sky," in the Vedic hymns, Aphrodite herself is often referred to by the exact cognate metrical formula *Dios thugatēr*, "daughter of Zeus," in the archaic Greek epics. These scholars claim that the goddesses' intimate textual affinity with the sky and the sky god is the decisive indication of their common heritage from an original Indo-European goddess of the dawn. However, more recent scholarship has tended to reject this theory regarding the supposed philological correlations between an Indo-European dawn goddess and the eventual Greek Aphrodite. Indeed, whatever evidence might exist about Indo-European mythology may have already been influenced by or integrated with Near Eastern and native Aegean mythological motifs and traditions. So perhaps the Greek Aphrodite may indeed reflect a complex combination of several chronological, cultural and geographical sources.

NAMES

What's in a name, and when did Aphrodite's name first appear in the Greek world? The name "Aphrodite" first occurs in Greece in the narrative poems of Homer and Hesiod, which were composed in the late eighth or early seventh century BC. Aphrodite is also named on the so-called "Nestor Cup" from Pithekoussai, a Greek colony or *emporion* (trading post) founded by Euboeans in the early eighth century BC on the island of Ischia off the western coast of Italy. A *kotylē*, or clay drinking cup, the "Nestor Cup" was discovered in 1954 during excavations of a grave containing objects dating to *ca.* 730–720 BC. Thus, the inscription is one of the oldest examples – as some would argue, *the* oldest example – of epigraphic writing using the ancient Greek alphabet.

"I am Nestor's cup, good for drinking.
Whoever drinks from this cup, immediately
Desire will seize him for beautiful-crowned Aphrodite."

("Nestor Cup" inscription, author's translation)

Yet new difficulties arise when we endeavor to analyze the authentic etymology of the name Aphrodite. Not surprisingly, this inquiry has provoked much controversy, where different scholars offer alternative linguistic rationales in the attempt to adapt the name Aphrodite to their favored theory of her cultural or geographical origins. Many proponents of the Indo-European origin of the goddess, for instance, take at face value that Aphrodite's name is fundamentally based on the Greek word *aphros*, following Hesiod's mythological description of her birth from the "sea foam" (*Theogony* 195–98). Certainly most early Greeks considered this to be the etymological basis of her name, and later writers (such as Plato, *Cratylus* 406c) naturally cited Hesiod as the source of this explanation. Hesiod reinforces his etymology by calling her *aphrogenēs*, or "foam-born" Aphrodite (*Theogony* 196). This epithet explicating the name Aphrodite has been further associated to her possible Indo-European origins as a dawn goddess, since some scholars connect the etymology of the Greek word *aphros* to conjectured Indo-European words for mist, fog, clouds and other types of natural moisture, and in particular to the Indic word *abrhá-*, or "cloud" (Boedeker 1974; Friedrich 1978). If her name is assumed to be a compound, then the second part has been explained as coming from the Greek word *hoditēs*, "wanderer," so the name would be Greek for "foam/cloud wanderer." Another suggestion is that the second element is built around the Indo-European root *dei-*, "to shine," with its related Greek adjective *dios*, "shining, bright, godlike," which would accord well with the frequent epithet of the goddess as *dia*, "shining," in early Greek poetry. Thus the name Aphrodite would mean something like "bright foam/cloud." A linguistic correlation with the Indo-European word component *dei-* would also link the goddess etymologically with the names of her Homeric "parents," Zeus and Dione. However, it must be noted that such scholarly efforts to establish a Greek or even Indo-European origin for Aphrodite's name have lately been dismissed as mere folk etymology.

More recent academic discourse argues that the name "Aphrodite" is not Greek nor is it even derived from any Indo-European language. Relying more broadly on the "orientalist" theory of the goddess' origin, some scholars maintain that the name Aphrodite is a Hellenic-accented appropriation of the name of one of her Near Eastern love-goddess antecedents. For example, some speculate that the goddess' Greek name is what most likely resulted when Greek speakers strained to get their mouths around the foreign syllables of the name Astarte, the Phoenician goddess. Other scholars agree that the name is genuinely Semitic, though they argue it is derived not from Astarte, but from another name or epithet of the goddess probably in use on the island of Cyprus where the Greek and Phoenician cultures first met (recently: West

2000). By analyzing the Semitic morphology and phonology of the name, a congruent hypothesis states that Aphrodite's name is a linguistic rendering into Greek of a possible local Cypriot-Phoenician cult title, *prāzit*, derived from *prāzi*, the Canaanite word for "country town," and so it would refer to the goddess as "Lady of the Villages." Other etymological interpretations of the divine name Aphrodite, some persuasive and some merely provocative, include Eteocypriot, Anatolian, Etruscan and Egyptian versions, as the debate continues to rage within scholarly circles.

Cypris and Cythereia

Like all the major deities of the Greek pantheon, Aphrodite was known by numerous cult titles, nicknames and literary epithets. Several of Aphrodite's most significant titles and epithets are linked to the various mythological stories of her birth and accounts of her origins. After the principal divine name Aphrodite, her most common titles in the Greek authors are *Cypris* and *Cythereia*, with both names ostensibly derived from those of the Mediterranean islands. These two epithets occur quite regularly in Greek literature, and so they suggest that Aphrodite can be easily identified with these islands, reflecting the fact that these were her most significant cult centers. Foremost is her title *Cypris*, "the Cyprian," which is widely used throughout ancient Greek poetry, along with the related forms *Cyprogenēs* and *Cyprogenea*, "Cyprus born." Aphrodite was also known by the epithet *Paphia*, "She of Paphos," alluding to her principal sanctuary at Paphos on Cyprus; the name occurs in some early archaic Cypriot inscriptions (Budin 2003). Thus, from very early on, these traditional literary and inscriptional epithets indicate Aphrodite's special relationship to the island of Cyprus, and perhaps suggest the substantial role played by the island in the development or transmission of the cult of Aphrodite from Paphos to the Greek mainland.

The name *Cythereia*, "the Cythereian," also appears to link the goddess to the island of Cythera, located just a few miles off the southern coast of the Peloponnese. Hesiod takes care to note that the newborn Aphrodite first approaches the island of the Cytherians on her way east to Cyprus, and hence earned the title *Cythereia* (*Theogony* 192–96). Other ancient Greek writers, including Herodotus (*The Histories* 1.105.2–3), support this association, claiming that Cythera was home to one of Aphrodite's earliest cult sanctuaries, which had been founded by roving Phoenicians. However, information gleaned from the archaeological record of early Cythera is inconclusive, with some traces of Near Eastern,

Egyptian and Minoan settlements on the island, but little in the way of specific Phoenician evidence (most recently, with review of evidence: Budin 2003). In fact, some scholars argue that the name *Cythereia* may originally have nothing at all to do with Aphrodite's famous cult on Cythera, as this particular title cannot be linguistically derived from the name of the island, due to the difference of vowel quantities evident in the two names (the island is *Cythēra*, while the goddess is *Cythĕreia*). Thus, it is suggested the name *Cythereia* may in fact be a feminine form of the name Kothar, a god of craftsmen in Ugaritic, an early language of Phoenicia (recently: West 1997). Since Kothar would correspond to Hephaestus in the Greek pantheon, this epithet may provide an explanation of Aphrodite's peculiar marriage to the Greek blacksmith god, as told in the song of Demodocus (*Odyssey* 8.266–366). According to this theory, after this early association was forgotten in Greek, writers like Hesiod and Herodotus attempted to account for the familiar title by connecting the goddess to the island of Cythera. Certainly the cult of the goddess on Cythera was well established by Hesiod's time.

Ourania

The name *Ourania*, "Heavenly," is the most frequently attested and widespread cult title for Aphrodite in the ancient Greek world (most recently, with overview of evidence: Rosenzweig 2004; also Pirenne-Delforge 1994). According to the testimony of the Greek writers, including Herodotus (*The Histories* 1.105) and Pausanias (*Description of Greece* 1.14.7), the goddess was celebrated as Aphrodite *Ourania* at her oldest and most sacred cult sanctuaries on Greek soil. The Greek authors also associate Aphrodite *Ourania* with the Phoenicians, who were said to have conveyed her cult worship to the Greeks. Thus, many scholars interpret this venerable cult title as an indication of Aphrodite's link to the Near Eastern love goddesses, in particular the Phoenician Astarte, who was known by the similar-sounding cult title "Queen of Heaven." Others construe the title as essentially a patronymic, arguing that the name *Ourania* originates from Aphrodite's relationship to her "father," the sky god Ouranos, as described in the Hesiodic account of her birth (*Theogony* 188–206). Though Hesiod never directly names her *Ourania*, the story of Aphrodite emerging from the sea and rising into the sky arguably emphasizes her celestial nature, which the title *Ourania* confirms.

But the fact that the name *Ourania*, the most well-known cult title for Aphrodite in Greece, is not used as a literary epithet in mythological accounts about the goddess has generated more scholarly speculation.

Some scholars argue that this indicates the name *Ourania* is clearly a cult epiclesis, that is, an inheritance from the sphere of cult rather than mythology. As such, the cult epithet *Ourania* had to be the historical condition that inspired the Hesiodic birth myth, that is, the title was already common in Greece at the time of Hesiod. Recent scholarship cites an early Near Eastern parallel for the myth of the castration of Ouranos and the subsequent birth of new deities: this is the creation story recounted in the *Song of Kumarbi* of the Hurrians, who lived in northern Mesopotamia during the late Bronze Age (Caldwell 1987). Thus, it is suggested that Hesiod's poetic imagination adapted the castration story to support his tale of Aphrodite's birth from the sky god's genitals, so that this Ouranian origin would account for her most recognizable and widespread epithet. Wherever she hails from, Aphrodite *Ourania*, whose cults and shrines are sprinkled throughout mainland Greece and the islands, is without question the most Panhellenic manifestation of the goddess.

OVERVIEW

In our examination of her literary, mythological and cultic beginnings, we discover that Aphrodite emerges as a deity of multiple layers and meanings. The mythological variants in the earliest Greek literary accounts of the goddess' birth expose key aspects of her manifold divine nature as imagined by the ancient Greeks. Likewise, the numerous and diverse theories of Aphrodite's possible ethnic, geographical and chronological origins, as suggested and promoted by both ancient writers and modern scholars, indicate that her development and diffusion as a figure of worship may exist on multiple yet concurrent levels. Finally, our inquiry into some of her most popular names and epithets reveal that Aphrodite's earliest literary myths and her most traditional cult places are inextricably bound together.

3
LOVE, SEX, WAR

In this chapter, we will consider the broad scope of Aphrodite's power as the goddess of love and sexuality. This chapter will elucidate how the goddess exemplifies the concept of *mixis*, the sexual mingling of bodies, in the imaginations of the ancient Greek writers. We will investigate the erotic implications of Aphrodite's connection to the concept of *peithō*, or persuasion, while also assessing the significance of her epithets *Pandēmos* and *Philommeidēs* and her association with the practice of prostitution. Next, this chapter will explore the relationship of the goddess to the love gods Eros and Himeros, who are often portrayed as her companions in Greek art, literature and myth. As the personification of sexual desire or lust, Eros represents the aggressive and covetous impulse towards erotic gratification. We will reflect on whether the ancient Greeks conceived of both Aphrodite and Eros as dangerous and even destructive agents of sexual passion. We will conclude this chapter by scrutinizing the claim that Aphrodite's divine nature may also encompass the realm of warfare, the mingling of bodies in battle.

LOVE AND SEX

Aphrodite appears in the earliest Greek texts as the goddess of love and sexuality, the deity who influences the negotiation and attainment of sexual pleasures for all sentient beings, including mortals and immortals, beasts and birds. The goddess exercises genial but absolute dominion over this subjective world of erotic engagement, a realm that the Greek writers like to call *ta aphrodisia*, literally "the things that belong to Aphrodite." In Hesiod's telling of her birth (*Theogony* 188–206), an early narrative account composed sometime in the eighth or seventh century BC, Aphrodite is said to have acquired this particular sphere of control immediately upon her emergence from the salty sea foam that sprang up around the severed genitals of Ouranos. Thus, the poet's tale of ambush and castration links Aphrodite to the violence and aggression that is inherent in the ancient Greek concept of the erotic experience (Carson 1986; Cyrino 1995), while Hesiod also implies that the birth of the beautiful goddess will initiate a new phase of more harmonious romantic encounters.

> From that moment on, among both gods and humans,
> She has fulfilled the honored function that includes
> Virginal sweet-talk, lovers' smiles and deceits
> And all of the gentle pleasures of sex.
>
> (*Theogony* 203–6, trans. Lombardo, 1993)

Even as Hesiod outlines the jurisdiction of Aphrodite's amatory power, the poet of the *Homeric Hymn to Aphrodite* (hymn 5) emphasizes the comprehensive scope of her authority. The fifth Homeric hymn offers another early demonstration of how the Greek poets viewed the goddess and her abilities, as it was probably composed sometime in the late seventh century (most recently, with review of scholarship: Faulkner 2008). In this hymn, Aphrodite is said to hold erotic sway over all living creatures in the world, except for the three sworn-virgin goddesses: Athena, Artemis and Hestia. So, apart from these three divine virgins, the hymn highlights the fact that no one else is able to escape Aphrodite's power to inspire sexual longing. Note how the hymn employs the inclusive language of the "polar expression" common among the archaic Greek poets to express the all-encompassing extent and totality of the goddess' control.

> Muse, tell what Aphrodite did once,
> The Cyprian who fills gods with sweet desire
> And tames the tribes of mortals while she's at it –
> And birds that cross the air, and beasts below them.
> The lovely-crowned Cytherean possesses
> All beings that the land and ocean nurture.
>
> (hymn 5.1–6, trans. Ruden, 2005)

Elsewhere in the early texts, however, Aphrodite sometimes needs to be reminded of the precise limits of her divine influence. The narrative motif of "putting Aphrodite in her place," either by establishing the exclusively erotic profile of her area of concern or by sharply delineating its exact boundaries, occurs with some frequency in her literary myths. Such a thematic recurrence may suggest the idea of the immense and

universal power wielded by Aphrodite was an abiding and traditional part of her mythological persona for the ancient Greeks (on the
"establishment of limits" motif: Bergren 1989; Clay 1989; Cyrino 1993).
One example of this motif occurs in book 5 of Homer's *Iliad*, where
Aphrodite is wounded on the battlefield when she tries to save her Trojan
son Aeneas from the rampaging Greek warrior Diomedes (5.311–51).
Upon her return to Olympus, Aphrodite is comforted by her Homeric
mother, Dione, while she is teasingly rebuked by her father, Zeus, for her
attempted exploits in the combat zone.

> The Father of Gods and Men smiled
> And calling Aphrodite said to her:
> "Dear child, war isn't your specialty, you know.
> You just take care of the pleasures of love
> And leave the fighting to Ares and Athena."
>
> (*Iliad* 5.426–30, trans. Lombardo, 1997)

All three of the above passages reveal how Aphrodite was granted an
undisputed place of prominence as the goddess of love and sexuality by
the earliest Greek writers. From the moment of her mythological birth to
her other appearances in the Greek tales, Aphrodite is the goddess who
rules over the erotic experience for all creatures of earth – human, divine
and animal – and we see how the all-embracing breadth of her dominion
is often underscored in the texts. The force of Aphrodite is what compels
sexual partners to join their bodies together in divinely inspired blending, as she induces them to blur their separate and individual boundaries until they merge together and become one. Aphrodite represents the
impulse towards intimate contact and fusion.

Míxis

The compulsion of Aphrodite demands *mixis*, a "mixing" or "mingling"
of bodies in a close physical transaction. For the ancient Greek writers,
mixis is the specific term used to describe the merging of bodies in
sexual intercourse: for example, Herodotus, the historian and nascent
anthropologist, uses the word when recounting the types of sexual intercourse engaged in by the various peoples he observes on his travels
(e.g. *The Histories* 1.203; 4.172). The noun *mixis* comes from the Greek
verb *mignumi* (sometimes spelled *meignumi*), which means "to mix,
mingle" or "to be brought into contact" with something in a close and
intimate manner. Indeed, in the early epic poems, *mignumi* regularly

carries two specific, but quite different, meanings: one is the mingling of bodies in battle, and the other is the mingling of bodies in sexual intercourse. The concept of *mixis*, "mingling," thereby connects or assimilates two usually very distinct areas of thematic significance, those of love and war. But as we continue to investigate the divine character of Aphrodite, these two areas may yet come together to reveal some of the crucial aspects that contribute to the nature of this complex goddess.

Homer uses the term to describe warriors "mixing it up" in battle, as when the Greek warrior Ajax rouses his men to tackle the Trojans: "Our only strategy is this: to take them on [*mignumi*] hand to hand, our muscle against theirs" (*Iliad* 15.509–10, trans. Lombardo, 1997). The verb is used in numerous other martial contexts to express the sweaty collision of fighters' bodies in combat (e.g. *Iliad* 4.456, 13.286, 21.469), or when an opponent is cut down, and a vital body part falls and "mingles" with the dirt on the ground (e.g. *Iliad* 10.457; *Odyssey* 22.329). In book 3 of the *Iliad*, the Trojan champion Hector uses the term in his stinging rebuke of his handsome but weak-willed younger brother Paris, Aphrodite's favorite, whose abduction of Helen started the whole war (3.38–57). Just before his scheduled duel with Menelaus, Helen's legal husband, Paris shrinks back in terror into the Trojan ranks, where Hector excoriates him for being bold when it comes to seducing women, but a coward on the battlefield.

"No, don't stand up to Menelaus: you might find out
What kind of man it is whose wife you're sleeping with.
You think your lyre will help you, or Aphrodite's gifts,
Your hair, your pretty face, when you sprawl [*mignumi*] in the dust?"

(*Iliad* 3.53–56, trans. Lombardo, 1997)

In this quotation, Hector combines the notions of love and war as he reprimands Paris for being a skilled connoisseur of one, and a doomed novice at the other. Such a collocation of the ostensibly opposed fields of love and war is reminiscent of the "make love, not war" passage in book 5 where Zeus chides Aphrodite for her failed effort to do battle with Diomedes, when she should just stick to her allotted realm of erotic pleasure (*Iliad* 5.426–30). Why does it make narrative sense, at least in the heroic world of epic poetry, to talk about love and war together? In both passages cited, the epic poet clearly articulates the apparent thematic proximity of these two concepts, love and war, while perhaps implying that the term of association is the idea of bodies sharing a vigorous but intimate physical exchange.

Elsewhere in the Homeric texts, the verb *mignumi* holds a more unambiguously sexual meaning (e.g. *Iliad* 3.445, 6.165, 14.295, 15.33, 24.131; *Odyssey* 1.433, 5.126, 11.268, 15.420, 22.445). One particular example occurs in book 9 of the *Iliad*, where the master negotiator, Odysseus, tries to convince a sullen Achilles to give up his anger against Agamemnon, and accept the king's offer of a ransom to return to the fighting (9.225–306): the payment includes gifts of precious metals, racehorses, beautiful women and the girl, Briseis, Achilles' prize, on whose account the conflict started when Agamemnon snatched her away. Here, the specific physical meaning of *mignumi* is the key proviso of the proposed reconciliation, as Odysseus promises that the girl remains sexually untouched by the king.

> "And with them will be the woman he took from you,
> Briseus' daughter, and he will solemnly swear
> He never went to her bed and lay with her [*mignumi*]
> Or did what is natural between women and men."
>
> (*Iliad* 9.273–76, trans. Lombardo, 1997)

The extent of Aphrodite's power to inspire erotic *mixis* "mingling" for both gods and humans, and even to mingle bodies across the ever-permeable boundaries between immortals and mortals, is abundantly illustrated in the mythological narrative of the *Theogony*. Hesiod, in his account of the generations of the Greek gods, frequently uses the verb *mignumi* as his preferred way of describing the sexual unions of various divinities, demigods and humans, and he often joins the verb to the phrase *en philotēti*, "in/with love," to highlight the erotic nature of these particular couplings (e.g. *Theogony* 920, 927, 941, 944, 970, 980, 1018); furthermore, he sometimes specifically names Aphrodite as the one who motivates the love making (e.g. *Theogony* 962, 980, 1014). Towards the end of his poem, Hesiod explains how even Aphrodite herself experiences the overwhelming drive towards sexual *mixis* – even across the divine/human border – when she desires the mortal Trojan cattleman, Anchises (the story is more fully told in the *Homeric Hymn to Aphrodite*, hymn 5).

> And Kythereia, beautifully crowned, bore Aineias,
> After mingling [*mignumi*] in sweet love with the hero Ankhises
> On the peaks above Ida's many wooded glens.
>
> (*Theogony* 1008–10, trans. Lombardo, 1993)

Where there is Aphrodite, then, there is *mixis*. The Greek writers portray the goddess as the divine source and inspiration for this erotic mingling, the ardent drive to couple together with another, and almost all living things are subject to the irresistible impulse aroused by this powerful deity. But how can such *mixis* be achieved? Sure enough, the goddess Aphrodite also holds sway over the realm of allure and seduction, that is, how to find, consummate and enjoy sexual blending to the fullest degree.

Peithō and Pandēmos

As the goddess of erotic mingling, Aphrodite is naturally associated with the various techniques, tactics and skills that draw lovers together: flirting and charm, cunning wiles, erotic deceits or "little white lies," and all the arts of seduction, allure and attraction. In this aspect of her power, Aphrodite is intimately linked to the workings of *peithō*, the Greek word for "persuasion, seduction, inducement." For the ancient Greeks, the concept of *peithō* carries both public and private connotations. While many Greeks (and, above all, the Athenians) would assert that the talents of persuasive speech are much sought after in the political and public arenas, it is the force of sexual persuasion in the private sphere that is most explicitly associated with the goddess Aphrodite. This erotic *peithō* governed by Aphrodite is manifest within the more personal milieus of amatory relationships, as well as in the familial and social celebrations of engagements and weddings. Thus, it is where these public and private spheres overlap that Aphrodite reveals to us her civic function: the goddess in her aspect as Aphrodite *Pandēmos*, the goddess who "belongs to all the people," presides over the harmonious unifica- tion of couples, households, and political factions that the workings of successful *peithō* can achieve.

Let us first investigate the crucial implications of erotic *peithō*, that is, how Aphrodite uses her power to unite lovers. Several examples in the earliest Greek texts demonstrate Aphrodite's formidable powers of sexual persuasion, and her capacity to merge lovers together. Perhaps one of the most famous episodes of her divine manipulation occurs in book 3 of the *Iliad*, where the goddess, after rescuing Paris from his ill- fated duel with Menelaus, induces Helen to join her Trojan lover in their palace bedroom. Readers of this passage have noted how the scene evokes the memory of, or even restages, the original *peithō* event in Sparta, when Aphrodite first persuaded Helen to leave her family and run away with Paris back to Troy (on the narrative strategy of "flash- back": Friedrich 1978; Nagy 1996). Now, deviously disguised as an old Spartan woman beloved by Helen, Aphrodite works her wiles once again as she coaxes Helen to go to meet the Trojan prince, as she draws an enticing tableau of Paris' physical beauty and athleticism waiting for her in their bed.

> "Over here. Paris wants you to come home.
> He's propped up on pillows in your bedroom,
> So silky and beautiful you'd never think
> He'd just come from combat, but was going to a dance,
> Or coming from a dance and had just now sat down."
>
> (*Iliad* 3.390–94, trans. Lombardo, 1997)

In this passage, we see how Aphrodite's skills of persuasion combine elements of deliberate trickery (or disguise), smooth speech and blatant temptation. Those are also features of the so-called *Dios Apatē* episode, or the "seduction/deception of Zeus," in book 14 of the *Iliad*, where the goddess Hera devises a plan to seduce her husband, the great god Zeus, to distract him away from the battlefield at Troy (*Iliad* 14.153–351). After adorning herself with glamorous perfume, clothing and jewelry to heighten her sexual magnetism, Hera seeks out Aphrodite, goddess of erotic persuasion, to solicit a favor that will add the ultimate ingredient to her allure, and cleverly begins her request with the following: "Might you be persuaded [*peithō*] by me?" (191). Hera asks Aphrodite to lend her the power of seduction, but she lies about its intended target (Zeus), pretending instead that she wants to reunite the quarreling Titan couple, Oceanus and Tethys: "If I can talk to them and have them make up [literally, 'persuade' them using *peithō*] – And get them together in bed again – They will worship the ground I walk on" (*Iliad* 14.208–10, trans. Lombardo, 1997). Aphrodite surely recognizes that Hera is telling a "little white lie" for a personal erotic purpose, as she indicates by her graceful consent to the queen of the gods.

> "How could I, or would I, refuse someone
> Who sleeps in the arms of almighty Zeus?"
> And with that she unbound from her breast
> An ornate sash inlaid with magical charms.
> Sex is in it, and Desire, and seductive
> Sweet Talk, that fools even the wise.
>
> (*Iliad* 14.212–17, trans. Lombardo, 1997)

Aphrodite's *kestos himas*, the "ornate sash" (214–15) or embellished leather strap the goddess wears around her upper body beneath her breasts, is the tangible piece of *accoutrement* that symbolizes her powers of persuasion, incorporating as it does all her skills of erotic enchantment ("magical charms," *thelktēria* 215), seductive flirtation ("Sweet Talk," *oaristus* 217) and sexual charisma ("Sex . . . and Desire," *philotēs* . . . *himeros* 216). With these tools at the ready, as Hera realizes in the *Dios Apatē* episode, Aphrodite is the definitive source of the power to unite lovers, even when they are separated (Zeus and Hera) or trapped in conflict (Oceanus and Tethys). The goddess uses her powers of persuasion to re-establish *mixis* in opposed couples.

The divine capacity of Aphrodite to achieve harmony between discordant lovers is also illustrated in the poetry of Sappho, who lived and composed exquisite verses in the city of Mytilene on the island of Lesbos around 600 BC. In what may be the only complete poem of her works to survive (poem 1), Sappho summons Aphrodite in very close and familiar terms, and begs the goddess to restore her to the good graces of an errant beloved. The poet dramatically portrays Aphrodite's playful yet convincing response to this request, as the goddess promises to use her compelling and persuasive influence to transform the beloved's reticence into absolute compliance.

> "Whom shall I persuade [*peithō*] this time
> to welcome you in friendship? Who is it,
> Sappho, that wrongs you?
>
> "For if she flees now, soon she shall pursue;
> if she refuses presents, she shall give them;
> if she does not love, soon she shall
> even against her will."

(poem 1.18–24, trans. Miller, 1996)

In Greek mythology, Peithō is also fully developed as a goddess in her own right, who was depicted by the ancient Greek artists and writers as the divine personification of persuasion. Hesiod says she is a daughter of Oceanus and Tethys, and so lists her among the Oceanids (*Theogony* 351); elsewhere, he notes that Peithō was one of the deities, along with the Charites or Graces – the customary attendants of Aphrodite – who helped adorn Pandora, the first mortal woman (*Works and Days* 73–74). In both Greek art and poetry, the goddess Peithō is often depicted as an attendant or companion of Aphrodite (most recently, with thorough review of ancient textual and artistic evidence: Rosenzweig 2004; Breitenberger 2007). The two are portrayed together in red-figure vase paintings of the late sixth century BC in scenes of the Judgment of Paris, where Peithō appears to be using her inherent skills of persuasion to influence the outcome of the mythical beauty contest in Aphrodite's inevitable favor. One of the most stirring portrayals in ancient Greek art of Aphrodite and Peithō together occurs on an *amphoriskos* by the Heimarmene painter (dated *ca.* 430 BC), depicting the moment just after the Judgment of Paris but before the abduction of Helen from Sparta. As Peithō stands nearby supervising the famous scene of persuasion, Aphrodite sits with her arm wrapped intimately around Helen, who is perched on the goddess' lap, hand on her chin as she contemplates her erotic destiny. On the other side of the seated duo waits Paris, striking in his heroic nudity, as a lithe winged Himeros (Desire) grips his arm and fixes him with an intense gaze. The composition of the scene suggests that between the seductive talents of Peithō and the irresistible physical attractions of Paris, Aphrodite will have no trouble in winning Helen over.

The people of Athens also associated the goddess Peithō with Aphrodite, chiefly with respect to Aphrodite's civic function as exemplified in her epithet *Pandēmos*, which means the goddess who "belongs to all the people" (most recently, with detailed survey of evidence and scholarship: Rosenzweig 2004). As an epithet or cult title, *Pandēmos* seems to have no Near Eastern parallel and instead appears distinctively related to the Athenian *polis*. Pausanias, the Greek travel writer, notes that Aphrodite and Peithō shared a cult site of great antiquity and importance on the southwest slope of the Athenian Acropolis (*Description of Greece* 1.22.3), where extant archaeological remains seem to confirm his observations. In cult, art and literature, the alliance of these two goddesses, Aphrodite *Pandēmos* and Peithō, symbolizes the concepts of unification and harmony in all of their public and private expressions. While Athenian statesmen might seek the joint endorsement of Aphrodite *Pandēmos* and Peithō to help unite opposing factions into political concord, yearning lovers or prospective brides would also look to these two beneficial and diligent goddesses to initiate erotic fusions and then shower their conjugal unions with blessings. *Peithō* is often understood as an epithet of Aphrodite herself, and sometimes the name is used to describe this specific aspect of Aphrodite's divine power to persuade, merge and unify. Thus, in looking at her complex relationship to Aphrodite, the multifaceted nature of Peithō emerges: she is both a goddess in her own right, and, at the same time, she represents a fundamental feature of Aphrodite's erotic power, that of sexual persuasion.

Philommeidēs

One of the most frequent literary epithets of Aphrodite is *philommeidēs*, and this particular title imparts a charming and sexually tinged *double-entendre* that seems appropriate to the goddess of love and sexuality (on the "multi-vocalism" of the epithet in archaic Greek poetry: Friedrich 1978). The recurrent epithet *philommeidēs* is used to describe Aphrodite numerous times in the Homeric epics (e.g. *Iliad* 3.424, 4.10, 5.375, 14.211, 20.40, and *Odyssey* 8.362), and several times in the *Homeric Hymn to Aphrodite* (hymn 5.17, 49, 56, 65, 155), as well as once in Hesiod's *Theogony* (989). As a composite form, the epithet *philommeidēs* follows one of the most common formulae for the formation of Greek compound nouns and adjectives, as it utilizes the verbal root *philo-*, meaning "to like, love, or be closely related to," preceding a second element referring to the item or activity liked, loved or related to: for example, the word *philosophos* would be rendered "lover of wisdom." Thus, the conventional translation of *philommeidēs* is "smile loving," based on the combination of *philo-* with the Greek verb *meidaō*, meaning "to smile," plus an agentive suffix *-ēs*; however, note that *philommeidēs* is also sometimes mistakenly translated as "laughter loving," thereby assigning a linguistically unsupported extension of the meaning of *meidaō*. Most translators follow accepted custom by rendering the description of the goddess as "smile loving" Aphrodite.

Supporters of the translation of *philommeidēs* as "smile loving" note that the goddess is often depicted smiling or associated with actual smiles in her early literary appearances (Boedeker 1974). For example, at the moment of her initial emergence from the sea foam, as Hesiod recounts the tale in the *Theogony*, Aphrodite is allotted "smiles" (*meidēmata*, 205) as one of her divine attributes. When Sappho makes her direct request to the goddess for erotic assistance in poem 1, the poet reminds Aphrodite how she once appeared to her "with a smile on your immortal face" (*meidiaisais'*, 1.14). Some would also argue that the epithet *philommeidēs* is not merely ornamental, but is intentionally employed in those literary contexts that emphasize Aphrodite's function as a goddess of sexual love. Thus, the epithet "smile loving" would convey explicitly erotic connotations, suggesting that Aphrodite's smile is in fact a calculated "come hither" gesture, one that is imbued with persuasive allure and has specifically sexual purpose.

A second translation of the epithet comes from another one of Hesiod's uses of the term, which is usually printed in most texts as *philommēdēs*, with the long vowel rather than the diphthong in the penultimate syllable of the epithet. In the *Theogony*, Hesiod offers a definite but very different etymology of the epithet during his description of Aphrodite's birth.

> Aphrodite
> Is her name in speech human and divine, since it was in foam
> She was nourished. But she is also called Kythereia since
> She reached Kythera, and Kyprogenes because she was born
> On the surf-line of Kypros, and Philommēdēs because she loves
> The organs of sex [mēdea], from which she made her epiphany.
>
> (*Theogony* 195–200, trans. Lombardo, 1993)

In his explication of Aphrodite's various epithets, Hesiod very clearly puts forth an interpretation that derives *philommēdēs* from the Greek epic plural noun *mēdea*, or "testicles, (male) genitals," and logically attributes this etymology to the emergence of the goddess from the castrated genitals of Ouranos. Hesiod's ingenious version seems to acknowledge that Aphrodite's birth from the sky god's genitals is an allegory for her intimate association with sexuality, in the same way Athena's birth from the head of Zeus connects her to the realm of the mind and wisdom. Whether Hesiod deliberately revised the goddess' traditional epithet *philommeidēs*, "smile loving," and replaced it with his own unique interpretation of the name is unclear, though many scholars tend to think that is exactly what the poet did. But perhaps the ancient pronunciation (in the oral tradition) and later spelling of the epithet were sufficiently ambiguous to allow Hesiod to take advantage of a play on words, both mythologically appropriate and psychologically appealing, wherein Aphrodite is allowed to be both her usual "smile loving" divine self, as well as the goddess who patently "likes, loves, and is closely related to the male genitals." Surely, such a *double-entendre* would make the goddess smile.

Prostitution

Since Aphrodite's essential divine function is erotic blending and sexual pleasure, it is not surprising to find her linked in the imaginations of the ancient Greeks to the activity of prostitution, what is sometimes called "the world's oldest profession" (most recently: Davidson 1997; Faraone and McClure 2006). Aphrodite is worshipped as the patroness and protector of prostitutes working at all levels of the sex trade: from the common, low-level whore, or *pornē*, who might typically be enslaved to a pimp or brothel-keeper and working for hire on the streets; to the glamorous, well-educated and elite-status courtesan, or *hetaira*, who would often run her own independent enterprise funded by one or more high-paying customers. Although it must be assumed that prostitution was known to the ancient Greeks from the earliest times, and no doubt Aphrodite as the goddess of sexual activity was at some early point in history aligned with the custom of commercial sex, the earliest Greek texts rarely mention the goddess in conjunction with the institution. The association between Aphrodite and prostitution in the Greek texts appears somewhat later and most conspicuously in the epigrams of the Hellenistic poets (composed primarily during the third and second centuries BC). In these short, witty poems, celebrated for their inscriptional brevity and clever insights, the topics of sexual love and erotic affairs emerge as principal themes. Several verses mention Aphrodite as the object of thank-offerings from appreciative "working girls" in exchange for the goddess' favor and success in their professions. An example of such a dedication is commemorated in this epigram by the poet Nossis (*ca.* third century BC), a native of Locri Epizephyri in Greek Italy, where there was an important shrine to Aphrodite.

> Let us go into the temple
> And look at the image of
> Aphrodite, curiously
> Wrought of gold. Polyarchis
> Gave it, from the rich harvest
> Of her own body's splendor.
>
> (poem 73, *Greek Anthology* 9.332, trans. Rexroth, 1999)

On the ancient Greek mainland, the most prominent center for the secular profession of prostitution was Corinth, a wealthy and lively city renowned – or rather notorious – for its commercial sex trade, or "erotic enterprise." Situated opportunely on the Isthmus, the narrow strip of land between mainland Greece and the Peloponnesus, ancient Corinth derived immense profit from the business traffic and trade that constantly passed through its boundaries, looking to take advantage of the quick and easy overland route through the city. With Corinth's busy commerce came merchants, economic officials and tourists of all kinds, who were eager to experience the city's extravagant amenities and attractions, especially its famously skilled and proverbially expensive prostitutes. The city's reputation as an exclusive hub for entrepreneurial sex at steep prices is attested in the popular proverb recorded by the Greek geographer Strabo (*ca.* 64 BC – AD 24): "Not for every man is the voyage to Corinth" (*Geography* 8.6.20). Several versions of this droll adage come down to us from antiquity, suggesting that luxury, commerce, money and prostitution were all elements of Corinth's unique appeal. Indeed, a modern twist on the saying might be: "What happens in Corinth, stays in Corinth." Ancient Corinth was also the site of a major temple to Aphrodite, located on Acrocorinth, the massive rocky acropolis high above the city proper, where there was a powerful and influential cult dedicated to the Greek goddess of love and sexuality (on the cult: Pirenne-Delforge 1994). A handful of ancient sources (such as Strabo, in the citation mentioned above) have been understood by some scholars to suggest that Aphrodite maintained in her sanctuary at Corinth a guild of "temple prostitutes," who would consecrate their earnings from any sexual transactions to the goddess. This notion of "cultic" or "sacred prostitution" in the service of Aphrodite at Corinth (and elsewhere) remains widespread in the contemporary popular imagination, such as in travel guides and websites, and can still be found in some older academic works on the subject of Greek religion. However, the current scholarly consensus is that "sacred prostitution" is essentially an historiographic myth, based on misunderstandings and deliberate misrepresentations on the part of the ancient sources alleging the practice, as well as critical mistranslations and other methodological problems in classical studies of the last century (most recently, with comprehensive analysis of evidence and scholarship: Budin 2008; also Pirenne-Delforge 1994, 2007). While there are no known first-hand accounts specifically describing the practice of "sacred prostitution" at Corinth, or anywhere else in the ancient world for that matter, a fragmentary verse of the archaic Greek poet Pindar (522–443 BC) is often proposed as evidence of some kind of ritual association between the Corinthian city prostitutes or courtesans and the goddess Aphrodite.

> Young women hospitable to many guests, attendants ,
> of Attraction [Peithō] in wealthy Corinth,
> you who burn the amber tears of blooming
> frankincense and often in your thoughts
> soar toward Aphrodite,
> the heavenly mother of desires,
> to you it has been granted, girls,
> without reproach on beds of love
> to pluck the fruit of your youth's delicate prime.
>
> (fragment 122.1–8, trans. Miller, 1996)

This is a fragment of a *skolion*, or "drinking song," that was composed by Pindar to commemorate the gratitude of Xenophon of Corinth after his

Olympic victory in 464 BC (he also commissioned Pindar to write an epinician ode, *Olympian* 13); it is preserved in the text of the Greek rhetorician Athenaeus (*Deipnosophistai* 13.573e–74b), who was writing around AD 200, and thus several hundred years after Pindar. In his introductory comments, Athenaeus tells us the poem celebrates Xenophon's conveying a group of "courtesans" (*hetairai*) to Aphrodite as a thank-offering for his victory. True, the first lines of the poem are addressed to "hospitable" *polyxenai*, young girls who are located in Corinth (1–2), and mention is made of burning incense to Aphrodite *Ourania*, "Heavenly" (5–6). But the song makes no explicit allusion to "sacred prostitution," nor to any permanent institutionalized dedication of courtesans to Aphrodite at her precinct in Corinth; nor does Pindar's Greek text ever specifically mention courtesans or prostitutes, sacred or otherwise, as he uses only neutral terms for the women (e.g. *neanides*, "young women" 1; *paides*, "girls" 7). Moreover, as a *skolion*, the fragment belongs to the symposiastic context rather than to any formal or ritual genre of religious dedication. Note, too, that the young women are called "attendants of Peithō", *amphipoloi Peithous* (1–2), highlighting their secular, professional talents to attract and seduce their customers. Thus, some scholars argue the possibility that Xenophon, in fulfillment of his vow at Olympia, invited or hired a bevy of expensive Corinthian courtesans for a thanksgiving feast or party at which this song was performed (Breitenberger 2007; Budin 2008). Yet might there still be some kind of ritual association between Xenophon's courtesans and Aphrodite at Corinth? No doubt they would also have made offerings to the goddess and participated in any regular or special cultic ceremonies in honor of Aphrodite in her sanctuary proper.

Indeed, while we may safely discount the specific practice of "sacred prostitution" as an historiographic myth, there is surely still an enduring religious connection between Aphrodite and the working girls of ancient Corinth, and everywhere else they plied their trade. Prostitutes and courtesans worshipped Aphrodite as an object of cultic veneration, and they could and did, like the Locrian courtesan Polyarchis, use their professional earnings to pay for sacral dedications and ritual celebrations in devotion to the goddess. Most notably, their very vocation of creating sexual pleasure in itself is an act of erotic blending that is always "sacred" to the goddess. Aphrodite *is* sacred sex.

Eros and Himeros

As the divine embodiment of erotic pleasure, Aphrodite is inextricably linked to Eros, the personification of sexual lust, in the imaginations of the ancient Greeks. The Greek noun *eros* describes the impulse of sexual desire, so Aphrodite's function as a goddess of love and sexuality necessarily hinges on the strength and influence of this universal drive. But *eros* is not just a sensation or instinct: the personified Eros is perceived by the ancient Greek writers and artists both as a primeval cosmic entity and as an individualized love god, while he is also often portrayed as subordinate to Aphrodite, either her attendant, companion or, later, even her son. The multivalence of Eros' mythological identity suggests that a variety of different literary and cultic traditions may have contributed to the way the ancient Greeks understood the figure of Eros (most recently, with thorough survey of ancient evidence: Breitenberger 2007). Just as Aphrodite's various birth stories suggest the many-layered nature of the goddess, the complexity of the figure of Eros is reflected in the multiple genealogies and affiliations proposed for him in the ancient Greek sources. For example, in Hesiod's cosmogonic narrative, Eros is one of the four primordial deities that emerge at the inception of time.

> In the beginning there was only Chaos, the Abyss,
> But then Gaia, the Earth, came into being,
> Her broad bosom the ever-firm foundation of all,
> And Tartaros, dim in the underground depths,
> And Eros, loveliest of all the Immortals, who
> Makes their bodies (and men's bodies) go limp,
> Mastering their minds and subduing their wills.
> (*Theogony* 116–22, trans. Lombardo, 1993)

Among the four cosmic principles, Eros is given the most developed description (120–22): Hesiod claims it is his unsurpassed beauty that gives him the power to overwhelm bodies and enthrall minds. Yet just a few verses later, Hesiod recounts how Eros joins the divine cohort of Aphrodite immediately after her appearance from the sea foam as one of her attendants, along with another deity, Himeros, the personification of yearning desire, or longing.

> Eros became her companion, and ravishing Desire [Himeros] waited on her
> At her birth and when she made her debut among the Immortals.
> (*Theogony* 201–2, trans. Lombardo, 1993)

While both love gods Eros and Himeros are regularly associated with Aphrodite, and they often appear together or separately in overtly erotic contexts, it is a bit tricky to differentiate between these two figures with precision. Based on the frequent usage of both terms in the ancient Greek texts, a discerning reader might be able to assign a certain nuance of meaning to distinguish the two: Eros may indicate a more physical, urgent condition of sexual desire for a love object that is directly within reach, whereas Himeros may denote a more emotional feeling of desire linked to the memory of an unavailable or inaccessible love object. In ancient Greek artistic representations, the iconography of Eros and Himeros also link the two figures to Aphrodite. One of the earliest images of Eros and Himeros occurs on an archaic Attic black-figure *pinax* (dated *ca.* 570–550 BC) found on the Athenian Acropolis, where a gaily dressed Aphrodite is shown carrying smaller-scale "baby" figures of Himeros and Eros in the crooks of her arms. The scene may be genealogical, implying that the two love gods are her children, or mythological, delineating the pair of key erotic zones under her divine influence. Numerous other images in Greek vase paintings depict Eros and Himeros as handsome winged youths in the company of Aphrodite in explicitly erotic settings, especially in wedding scenes, or in scenes illustrating the goddess' birth from the sea (most recently, with an excellent set of plates and interpretation: Rosenzweig 2004). The wings of Eros and Himeros, as with other pennate Greek deities, clearly suggest both the velocity of their onset and their ability to move swiftly between immortal and mortal realms to accomplish Aphrodite's will, while their youthful physical beauty suggests their irresistible allure.

Whenever they appear in the earliest Greek texts doing the work of Aphrodite, Eros and Himeros are both portrayed as powerful, aggressive, and even violent forces of erotic assault followed by total subjugation, inflicting bodily injury and madness upon poor lovers (on ancient Greek poetic notions about the damage wrought by the erotic experience: Carson 1986; Cyrino 1995). The Greek lyric poets, in particular, viewed the phenomenon of erotic desire as dangerously compelling, one that is hostile in intent and unpredictable in effect, and ultimately devastating, as they frequently use metaphors of war, conquest, captivity, fire, flood, storms, disease, insanity, and even death to describe the onset of love. One example of this notion of destructive desire – among the scores that can be cited – is found in the verses of Ibycus, a western Greek poet who was active in the second half of the sixth century BC. In this fragment, Ibycus contrasts the calm, seasonal regularity of nature with the severely erratic turmoil of Eros.

In spring the Kydonian
apple trees, watered by flowing
streams there where the Maidens
have their unravished garden, and vine buds,
growing under the shadowy branches
of the vines, bloom and flourish. For me, however, love [*eros*]
is at rest in no season,
but like the Thracian north wind
ablaze with lightning,
rushing from Aphrodite with scorching
fits of madness, dark and unrestrained,
it forcibly convulses, from their very roots,
my mind and heart.

(fragment 286.1–13, trans. Miller, 1996)

For Ibycus, Eros strikes like a hot, dry tempest, a thunderstorm without the relief of rain, bringing mental confusion and physical trauma. Moreover, in this verse Eros emanates directly from Aphrodite and acts as her agent, and elsewhere he is explicitly shown as her ally and accomplice in their joint campaign: in another poem of Ibycus, Eros wields his dark, alluring gaze to beguile the trembling lover and entice him into Aphrodite's inextricable nets (fragment 287). Both Eros and Aphrodite are experts at enchantment and seduction for the purpose of erotic *mixis*, to entangle lovers together, whether they are willing or not.

Nowhere is the multifaceted, complicated and intimate relationship between the goddess Aphrodite and her companion/accomplice Eros more remarkably expressed than in Euripides' tragic play *Hippolytus* (on the play: Barrett 1964; Goff 1990; Mills 2002). In the narrative of this play, an astonishing exposé of the destructive nature and drive of erotic desire, Aphrodite is set on revenge against the ascetic youth Hippolytus, who refuses sex and thus denies her divine power. The goddess causes the boy's stepmother, Phaedra, to fall madly in love with him, thereby initiating a disastrous trajectory leading to the death of Hippolytus at the hands of his father, the Athenian hero Theseus: that Phaedra's suicide comes along the way is considered merely collateral damage to Aphrodite's vengeful purpose. As the action of the play proceeds, the local women of the chorus ponder the volatile approach of erotic desire, as in this choral ode, where Eros is called the "child of Zeus" (534). Here Eros is represented as the ballistic instrument of Aphrodite, and the eager purveyor of her powerful celestial munitions.

Eros, Eros, melting desire in the eyes,
sweet delight in the souls
of all your victims,
come to me never, never if not in peace;
never upset my mind,
dance with me out of time.
Shafts of fire, piercing light of the stars
cannot compare with the bolt
of Aphrodite;
the bolt you fling from your hands,
Eros, child of Zeus.

(*Hippolytus* 525–34, trans. Svarlien, 2007)

In a later ode, the chorus of the *Hippolytus* portrays Aphrodite and Eros working together in treacherous tandem to dominate the entire world. The playwright Euripides follows the poet of the *Homeric Hymn to Aphrodite* in expressing the extent of the goddess' divine authority by using the archaic polar expression. Yet here he expands the description to include the winged Eros as her partner and an enthusiastic agent of her erotic control: his wheeling flight surveys the far-reaching totality of their dominion.

You, Aphrodite, move what cannot be swayed:
the steely minds of the gods
and of all mankind
rapt beneath the wing of the one who flies with you,
brilliant and sudden. Over the earth he soars;
he skims the tops of the waves
in the echoing surf.
Eros, flashing with gold, in a rush of beating wings
drives every heart insane:
the beasts who dwell in the mountains,
the creatures of the ocean,
all that the earth gives life to,
all the bright sun looks down on,
and every man.
Cypris, you alone
rule over all of these.

(*Hippolytus* 1268–82, trans. Svarlien, 2007)

While Aphrodite and Eros are associated with each other as deities of love and sexuality in early Greek art and literature, the popular image of Aphrodite as the mother of the little boy Eros is quite late, and evidently is influenced by the Roman poets and artists, who bequeathed the mother–son dyad to subsequent Western cultures. Earlier Greek poets, as noted above, offer several different parentages and genealogies for Eros, though no actual early text survives that unambiguously connects Eros to Aphrodite in a filial relationship. But since the Greek poets tend to subordinate facets of the major gods as their assistants or children, it is quite possible that one or more of these early poets did make Eros the son of Aphrodite. For instance, a commentator on a later Greek text notes that Sappho in her poetry makes Eros the child of Aphrodite and Ouranos (*scholium* on Theocritus, *Idyll* 13); if accurate, this suggests Sappho may be combining the love god's two Hesiodic aspects: Eros the cosmic element, and Eros the near intimate of the goddess of love. Another later commentator quotes a poorly preserved couplet by the lyric poet Simonides of Ceos (*ca.* 556–468 BC), where he appears to call Eros the "cruel child," *schetlie pai*, of Aphrodite and Ares, the god of war, Aphrodite's favorite lover (fragment 575.1, *scholium* on Apollonius of Rhodes, *Argonautica* 3.26): if the text is not corrupt, this pedigree would make Eros the offspring resulting from the familiar tale of his parents' divine adultery told in book 8 of Homer's *Odyssey*. These various genealogies signal the complexity of Eros' mythological identity for the early Greeks.

But the first clear-cut textual depiction of Eros as the young child of Aphrodite occurs in book 3 of the *Argonautica*, the heroic tale of Jason's quest for the Golden Fleece, written by Apollonius of Rhodes at Alexandria in the third century BC. Book 3 recounts the love affair between the hero, Jason, and the fairy princess, Medea, daughter of Aietes, the king who controls the magic fleece. As the book opens, the goddess Hera, who supports Jason's quest, asks Aphrodite to persuade her "son" *pais* (so designated by Hera with possessive pronouns at 3.26, 85 and 110) to shoot his inescapable arrows into the princess to charm her with love for Jason, so that she will help him accomplish his heroic goals. Aphrodite consents, and thus cajoles her "greedy" *margos* boy (3.120), Eros, to take up the task, with the promise of a fabulous toy that once belonged to baby Zeus: a round ball *sphaira* (3.135) magnificently fashioned with gold zones and dark-blue spirals, that when tossed in the air leaves a fiery comet trail (3.128–45). The poet's detailed description of the ball evokes the image of the globe or cosmos, and its transmission from Olympian Zeus to Eros indicates the love god's unmistakable aspiration to control the entire universe as its supreme deity: note how Euripides' Eros soars possessively over the whole earth (*Hippolytus* 1272). As expected, Eros is both delighted and instantly aroused by the bribe.

He threw down all his toys and with both hands clutched hold firmly to the side of the goddess' tunic; he begged her to give the ball to him at once, there and then. She spoke softly to him, drew his cheeks towards her and kissed him as she held him. With a smile she said to him:

> "Be witness now your own dear head and mine! I swear to give you the gift and not to deceive you, if you shoot your arrow into Aietes' daughter."

At these words he gathered up his knucklebones, carefully counted them, and threw them into his mother's shining lap.

(Argonautica 3.146–55, trans. Hunter, 1993)

This appealing passage encapsulates many features of the close and complex rapport between Aphrodite and Eros, her collaborator, *consigliere*, and dearly loved but spoiled child. To the ancient Greek writers and artists, Aphrodite and Eros represent an indissoluble alliance engaged in the relentless project of bringing about sexual *mixis*, the erotic merging of bodies, by persuasion, seduction, coercion, or even force, if necessary. Perhaps it is this aggressive nature of erotic desire, and the impulsive belligerence embodied by the personified Eros, who is often in Greek poetry imagined as Aphrodite's love child by the war god Ares, that suggests her association to the realm of warfare.

WAR

One of the most controversial topics in the scholarly endeavor to understand the nature of Aphrodite is the role of militarism in the portrayal of the goddess, and the relationship of warfare to the more familiar areas under her influence and control, especially love and sexuality (most recently, with wide-ranging survey of data: Pironti 2007; Budin 2009). While she is surely not considered a deity of warfare like Ares or Athena, nevertheless Aphrodite does not shy away from the combat zone. In book 5 of the *Iliad*, Homer relates how Aphrodite rushes to enter the fray to save her son Aeneas on the Trojan battlefield, where she is attacked and wounded by the fierce Greek warrior Diomedes.

> Diomedes knew
> This was a weakling goddess, not one of those
> Who control human warfare – no Athena,
> No Enyo here, who demolishes cities –
> And when he caught up to her in the mêlée

He pounced at her with his spear and, thrusting,
Nicked her on her delicate wrist, the blade
Piercing her skin through the ambrosial robe
That the Graces themselves had made for her.

(*Iliad* 5.331–38, trans. Lombardo, 1997)

Though Diomedes gets the better of her in this encounter, and her father, Zeus, later reminds her that her particular province of expertise is love, not war (5.426–30), what is often overlooked here is Aphrodite's willing incursion into the bloody fighting to rescue her son. In fact, we should ask why the goddess of love should even feel comfortable on the battlefield, and why she would rush headlong into a skirmish she knows she might lose. In Greek mythology, Aphrodite's favorite lover is Ares, god of war: in the combat scene in book 5 of the *Iliad*, she borrows Ares' chariot to ride back to Olympus after she is hurt (5.350–62). Later, in the *Theomachia* episode of book 21, when the gods are all at each other's throats, Aphrodite is quick to help a wounded Ares off the field of combat (21.416–17). Greek myth also allots Aphrodite as wife to Hephaestus, the blacksmith god, who makes armor and weapons used in war, including an extraordinary new shield for the warrior Achilles (*Iliad* 18.478–608). Aphrodite herself is the instigator of the Trojan War, the most famous military campaign in all of Greek mythology: it was her divine influence that compelled the *mixis* of the adulterous couple Paris and Helen. Thus, even if Diomedes considers her a "weakling" *analkis* (5.331), it appears Aphrodite does have some genuine experience in the arena of warfare.

While some traces of evidence suggesting Aphrodite's link with militarism do indeed surface in her ancient Greek cultic, artistic and literary appearances, needless to say, these clues tend to be ambiguous and even contradictory, and thus prone to academic speculation, debate and controversy. Questions regarding her martial character focus on whether Aphrodite herself is portrayed as a warrior engaged in active combat or whether she serves as an inspiration for other fighters or possibly leads them into battle; also, it is a challenge to identify the probable origins or underlying source for these warlike aspects in her divine character. Some scholars believe that Aphrodite's martial persona, if indeed she has one, is most likely a remnant of the early or lingering influence on her origins of the Near Eastern goddesses associated with both sexuality and warfare, such as Ishtar (Flemberg 1991); later, according to these scholars, Aphrodite was "stripped" of this militaristic component and became solely a goddess of love. Still other scholars argue that Aphrodite's associations with militarism emerge directly out of her developed Greek persona as the goddess of violent sexuality who presides over the clashing together of bodies in erotic *mixis* (Pironti 2007). Thus, just as problems abound in determining Aphrodite's geographic, ethnic and chronological origins, it is no easy task to establish an ultimate derivation for any martial attributes apparent in her character.

Some evidence points to possible militaristic elements in Aphrodite's cults and shrines, though most of these attestations are rather late (most recently, with thorough survey of data and scholarship: Budin 2009). For example, the travel writer Pausanias, working in the second century AD, mentions three times the existence of "armed" (*hoplismenē*) Aphrodite statues in Greece: at Cythera (*Description of Greece* 3.23.1), Corinth (2.5.1) and Sparta (3.15.10). While Pausanias follows Herodotus (*The Histories* 1.105) in asserting that Cythera was a major center for the worship of Aphrodite from very early antiquity, he doesn't provide any more detailed information about the cult statue he simply describes as an armed *xoanon* or wooden statue of the goddess. At Corinth, which was completely razed by the Romans in 146 BC and rebuilt by Julius Caesar in 44 BC, what Pausanias likely saw was a statue of the Roman goddess and Caesar's divine forebear, Venus Victrix, "She who Conquers," rather than an image of the Greek Aphrodite.

Of all her early cults, it is most probable that Aphrodite may have manifested a military persona in archaic and classical Sparta. In addition to Pausanias' report of a *xoanon* of Aphrodite Hoplismenē housed in an ancient temple there (3.15.10), a few Hellenistic epigrams from the third century BC (and later) depict the specifically martial aspect of the Spartan Aphrodite (e.g. *Greek Anthology* 9.320, 16.176). Even more interesting is Pausanias' description of another temple in Sparta dedicated to Aphrodite Areia (3.17.5). This cult, supported by independent epigraphical data from the late Archaic period, suggests Aphrodite was worshipped at Sparta as a female Ares, "Areia." But it is not clear whether Aphrodite Areia herself bore arms as a warrior or was revered in a joint cult with her more warlike paramour, Ares. Such joint cults of Aphrodite and Ares are found elsewhere in Greece and Crete, yet nowhere in these cults does Aphrodite display a distinctly martial aspect. Indeed, scholars note that the joint cults of Aphrodite and Ares most likely celebrate the gods as conflicting yet connected forces, love and war, linked by the notion of *mixis*, the intensely physical merging of bodies (Pirenne-Delforge 1994; Pironti 2007). Aphrodite engages in war to the extent that the divine lovers perform *mixis* in their mythological and cultic appearances.

Thus, a handful of evidence suggests Aphrodite may have had some militaristic aspects to her persona at a few early sites in Greece: for example, the description of her sacred statues as "armed" or her cult at Sparta as "Areia." And while we grant that some ancient Greeks may have recognized warlike elements in Aphrodite's divine nature, it seems that her military attributes, if any, were eventually downplayed when she emerged as a fully developed Olympian goddess. In book 5 of the *Iliad*, Zeus tells her "war isn't your specialty," but we have also seen that Aphrodite doesn't avoid the battlefield. Yet whatever hints of the warrior Aphrodite may surface in the ancient archaeological and literary records, most scholars agree that the image of a militaristic Aphrodite does not represent the prevailing or traditional Greek portrayal of the great goddess of love and sexuality.

OVERVIEW

Our survey of Aphrodite's most significant realm of authority, love and sexuality, confirms she is a goddess of immense and universal power, and her influence is exemplified in her epithets *Pandēmos* and *Philommeidēs*. Aphrodite inspires *mixis*, and her association with the concepts of *peithō* and the practice of prostitution demonstrate crucial aspects of her divinity as imagined by the ancient Greeks. Most importantly, Aphrodite's relationship with the love gods, Eros and Himeros, indicates there is an extraordinary level of complexity inherent in the way the ancient Greeks understood the experience of sexual desire. It is this violent and aggressive longing for *mixis* that links Aphrodite to her lover, Ares, and suggests a possible warlike aspect for the goddess of erotic love. The motto of such a deity would then be: "Make love *and* war."

4

BEAUTY, ADORNMENT, NUDITY

In this chapter we will explore the significance of Aphrodite as the ancient Greek goddess of beauty. We will consider the various aspects of Aphrodite's connection to the concept of physical attractiveness as well as the processes of beautification and decoration for the purpose of enhancing erotic appeal. In particular, we will reflect on Aphrodite's close iconographic association to the quality of goldenness, and her link to gold ornaments, attributes and jewelry. This chapter will also survey some of the minor goddesses and divine personifications who accompany and surround Aphrodite, adorning her like a garland of animate beauty. We will conclude with a consideration of nudity as an articulation of the goddess' power and an important dimension of her physical beauty, by regarding its artistic expression in Praxiteles' famous statue, the Aphrodite of Knidos.

BEAUTY

The ancient Greek writers and artists imagined Aphrodite as the embodiment of the ideal of feminine beauty, as she both exhibits and exemplifies an incomparable loveliness that is utterly and inextricably fused with the nature of her divinity. Indeed, all the major Greek goddesses are portrayed as being beautiful in their physical appearance, and each one boasts particular features and diverse attributes that enhance her personal charisma: Artemis is distinguished by her height, Athena by her noble bearing, and Hera by her luminous skin (Friedrich 1978). But the standard Greek adjective used to designate what is "beautiful," *kalē*, belongs especially to Aphrodite. In the iconography of Greek art, cult, myth and literature, Aphrodite's physical beauty is most often portrayed in terms of a "pre-maternal" womanhood: her body type is usually depicted as young, slim, fresh and rounded, that is, the female figure at the perfect peak of maturity, without the fuller, more nutritive features that tend to signify the mother goddess Demeter (Breitenberger 2007). The poet Sappho (*ca.* 600 BC) describes Aphrodite as "slender" *bradina* (fragment 102.2). Aphrodite's perfectly ripened beauty defines the essential, ideal moment in the representation of female physical excellence, as she embodies the epitome of what it means to be at the height of one's powers of erotic attraction and allure.

Aphrodite's image as the goddess of erotic beauty is explicitly supported by her appearances in early Greek poetry, where there emerges an almost voyeuristic interest in the specific characteristics of her awe-inspiring physicality. In the earliest poems and texts, the beauty of Aphrodite is described with careful attention to detail, and with overt references to the many glorious qualities of her physical attributes. If we understand the goddess' frequent epithet *philommeidēs* in its traditional interpretation, then Aphrodite is customarily portrayed in the early texts wearing a smile, an alluring facial gesture that imparts both prettiness and sexual magnetism to her countenance: as Sappho describes the goddess' chariot-drawn arrival, "with a smile on your immortal face" (poem 1). The stunning Aphrodite is also often described in Greek poetry as having dazzling eyes, an exquisite-looking neck, and a lovely décolletage. These signature divine features, according to the poets, are so divinely radiant and so powerfully attractive, that a few perceptive mortals can immediately recognize them even when the goddess dons a disguise. This is exactly what Helen does in book 3 of Homer's *Iliad*, when a cleverly camouflaged Aphrodite tries to lure the Spartan queen to join her lover, Paris, in bed.

> She [Helen] knew
> It was the goddess – the beautiful neck,
> The irresistible line of her breasts,
> The iridescent eyes. She was in awe . . .
>
> (*Iliad* 3.396–98, trans. Lombardo, 1997)

Here, Aphrodite's neck is "beyond beautiful" (*perikallēs*, 396); her bosom is so lovely that it "inspires *himeros*" or "longing" (*himeroenta*, 397); and her eyes literally "flash fire" (*marmairō*, 397), a verb used by the Greek poets elsewhere to describe light glinting from metal (of Achilles' new armor: *Iliad* 18.617), or the gleam of cosmic phenomena (of Zeus' thunderbolt: Hesiod, *Theogony* 699). Thus Aphrodite's beauty is made manifest by the poets in explicit textual description, while being revealed in terms of its effect on the observer: her supernatural beauty arouses desire in beholders and dazzles them with her sparkling divinity.

In book 18 of the *Odyssey*, Homer accentuates this tendency towards descriptive specificity in Aphrodite's association to physical beauty, in an episode where Penelope, wife of Odysseus and queen of Ithaca, appears before the suitors. Although Penelope refuses her maid's suggestion that she bathe and put on cosmetics to improve her good looks and thus impress the avid men gathered in her hall, the goddess Athena intervenes and beautifies the queen as she sleeps, by applying the "immortal beauty" (*kallei . . . ambrosiōi*, 192–93) that belongs to Aphrodite.

> Then the shimmering goddess [Athena] went to work on her [Penelope],
> So that all the men would gape in wonder.
> First she cleansed her lovely face, using
> The pure, distilled Beauty that Aphrodite
> Anoints herself with when she goes garlanded
> Into the beguiling dances of the Graces.
> Then she made her look taller, and filled out her figure,
> And made her skin whiter than polished ivory.
>
> (*Odyssey* 18.190–96, trans. Lombardo, 2000)

It is unclear whether Aphrodite's "immortal beauty" (192–93) referred to in this passage is meant to be the abstract concept of beauty, *kallos*, that the goddess readily bestows upon her favorites; or some more tangible substance, like a restorative balm or unguent, such as the "immortal oil" used by the Graces to anoint Aphrodite in her sanctuary at Cyprus before her seduction of the Trojan cattleman Anchises (*elaiōi ambrotōi*: *Theogony* 61–62): indeed, many modern women today trust in the "immortal" properties of curative, beautifying and age-reversing creams and ointments. However, Aphrodite's "immortal beauty" appears to be something that can be borrowed, used and applied by others, as Athena does in this episode for the purpose of enhancing Penelope's physical allure and to fill the suitors with sexual desire; a similar "borrowing" event occurs in the *Dios Apatē* episode in book 14 of the *Iliad*, when the goddess Hera meticulously adorns herself to seduce her husband, Zeus, and then asks Aphrodite to lend her the magic love charm, an embellished sash worn beneath the breasts (*kestos himas*, 14.214–15), as the finishing touch to her erotic attractiveness. Whatever the exact nature of this "immortal beauty" and the mode of its application, the beautification of Penelope's specific features listed one by one in the *Odyssey* passage closely corresponds to the direct enumeration of Aphrodite's physical attributes elsewhere in Greek poetry. With beauty from the goddess, Penelope's figure becomes taller and more rounded (*makroterēn kai passona*, 18.195), while the surface of her body is brightened to an incandescent luster ("whiter . . . than buffed ivory," *leukoterēn . . . pristou elephantos*, 196). Explicitness in physical description, then, is a characteristic of the literary iconography of Aphrodite, as well as those mortal females who are blessed, however temporarily, with her beauty.

But to praise a mortal woman's beauty most vividly, even when the description itself is not precise or detailed, the Greek poets will simply compare her to Aphrodite. In doing so, the poets often employ the formulaic phrase containing the goddess' distinctive epithet "golden," *chruseē*. This epithet has clear and specific reference to Aphrodite's physical appearance, and the phrase "golden Aphrodite" is used in many contexts where the theme of her beauty is emphasized (Boedeker 1974: more on the meaning of this epithet below). Thus the phrase occurs appropriately as part of the traditional way of extolling a mortal woman's beauty in the epic texts. For example, in book 4 of the *Odyssey*, Homer describes Helen's "lovely" daughter Hermione, "who had the looks of golden Aphrodite" on her wedding day (4.13–14). Elsewhere in the *Odyssey*, both before and after the divine beautification scene illustrated above, Penelope is twice described as "looking like golden Aphrodite" (17.37, 19.54). In the *Iliad*, the captive girl Briseis, when she is returned to the warrior Achilles, is described as "looking like golden Aphrodite" (19.282). At the end of the epic, the Trojan princess Cassandra is described as "looking like golden Aphrodite" (24.699). Earlier, in book 9 of the *Iliad*, Achilles puts an angry spin on the formulation when in exchange for his return to battle, he refuses the Greek ransom gifts and, in particular, the offer of a family alliance with Agamemnon: "I would not marry the daughter of Agamemnon, son of Atreus, not even if she rivaled golden Aphrodite in beauty" (9.388–89). So when Helen appears, dressed in gleaming white linens, on the Trojan ramparts in the *Teichoskopia* episode in book 3 of the *Iliad*, and the Trojan elders judge her facial countenance to be "strikingly like the immortal goddesses" (3.158), there is no doubt as to which goddess they mean.

ADORNMENT

As the epitome of feminine beauty, Aphrodite effortlessly expands her divine influence to encompass the use of physical adornment to boost sexual magnetism and achieve erotic goals. Thus the goddess can be said to symbolize the notion of "beauty enhanced for a purpose." The Greek writers and artists often portray Aphrodite in scenes of *kosmēsis*, "adornment," where the goddess is shown in the process of augmenting her magnificent natural beauty with various strategies of decoration for the face, body and hair, such as fine clothing, jewelry, headbands, fragrance and cosmetics. Collectively, these enhancements are known as the *kosmos*, "ordering, arrangement, outfit, make-up," that typically belongs to a female figure (e.g. *kosmos* pertaining to Hera's adornment: *Iliad* 14.187; of Pandora's apparel: Hesiod, *Works and Days* 76); note the Greek word *kosmos* is the obvious source for our modern word "cosmetics." Moreover, such scenes depicting Aphrodite's *kosmēsis* or "*toilette*" often occur in narratives of seduction and erotic pursuit that emphasize her function as a deity of sexuality, so that the two concepts, love/sex and beauty/adornment, are portrayed as intimately linked in the imaginations of the ancient Greeks.

Scenes of Aphrodite's personal embellishment occur in several early Greek texts, and these passages notably exhibit an exuberant and exhaustive attention to detail within an inventory format. The *Homeric Hymn to Aphrodite* (hymn 5), which was probably composed sometime in the late seventh century BC, offers perhaps the most remarkable depiction of Aphrodite's adornment in early Greek literature (most recently, with careful review of scholarship: Faulkner 2008). In the narrative of this hymn, the poet describes how Aphrodite is smitten with desire for the mortal Trojan cattleman Anchises; after first seeing him on Mt. Ida in Troy, the goddess goes directly to her temple on the island of Cyprus to prepare herself to seduce him (53–57). Scholars note that this hymnic scene of Aphrodite's *kosmēsis*, set in her island shrine at Paphos, reveals the goddess in the act of assuming her unique divine powers of attraction and seduction, and some suggest that this literary epiphany may even reflect actual cult ritual in numerous respects (most recently, with extensive survey of evidence: Breitenberger 2007). In her favorite island sanctuary, surrounded by her special attendants, the poet of the hymn illustrates how the goddess Aphrodite literally embodies the ideal of erotic beauty and allure.

> The Cyprian shrine at Paphos, full of incense,
> Features her holy ground and fragrant altar.
> She went there, went inside, and shut the bright doors.
> And there the Graces bathed her and rubbed on her
> A holy oil that blooms on the undying –
> She kept this heavenly-sweet perfume handy.
> Now dressed in every kind of gorgeous garment
> And gold-festooned, fun-loving Aphrodite
> Left fragrant Cyprus – straight to Troy she headed.

> (hymn 5.58–66, trans. Ruden, 2005)

But the most detailed description of her splendid adornment is delayed in the text until its effect upon the mortal Anchises can be elaborated. In a fine trick of appearance, both to arouse the man's desires and allay his fears, Aphrodite assumes the disguise of a young mortal virgin (81–83). At this real-time moment of presentation in the human realm, all the descriptive elements of Aphrodite's earlier *kosmēsis* in the temple at Paphos are developed and amplified as they are perceived by Anchises, while specific emphasis is given to each individual piece of her profusion of glittering jewelry.

> Anchises looked her over in amazement:
> So tall, well-built, and radiantly dressed! –
> The robe more brilliant than a flash of fire,
> Coiled brooches and bright earrings shaped like flowers.
> Around her delicate neck was lovely jewelry
> Of gold, ornately worked. As the moon glimmers,
> So her young bosom marvelously glimmered.
>
> (hymn 5.84–90, trans. Ruden, 2005)

In this scene, the theme of divine epiphany is linked to the ornamentation motif, as Aphrodite presents herself to Anchises as an ambiguously divine-looking maiden of impressive and well-appointed beauty. Aphrodite's lavish *accoutrement*, like the sheer loveliness of her face and body visible beneath the trinkets, becomes manifest in the poetic descriptions at the moment of perception by the awestruck observer. Thus, the epiphany of the goddess to her lover in the fifth Homeric hymn, with all her physical beauty and adornment, is more than just a tale of attraction: the narrative underscores Aphrodite's divine power by defining her specific function as a deity and delineating the exclusive spheres of her influence – charm, enticement and seduction.

Another adornment scene is embedded within an account of Aphrodite's birth from the sea in the sixth Homeric hymn. The poet opens this short hymn with an evocation to the goddess in her elemental island milieu: "I'll sing of gold-crowned, lovely Aphrodite, honored owner of Cyprian battlements, set in the sea, where the wet-gusting west wind and the soft-foaming, racketing waves bestowed her" (hymn 6.1–4, trans. Ruden, 2005). As in the Hesiodic birth narrative (*Theogony* 188–206), the goddess is invested with her supernatural powers at the moment of her arrival on the beach. In the sixth Homeric hymn, there follows an exquisitely detailed description of Aphrodite's dressing and ornamentation by a group of attendant minor goddesses – in this case, the *Horae*, or Hours – as Aphrodite is shown to assume her allotted attributes of beauty, embellishment and erotic allure just after she emerges from the water.

> On shore, the Hours in their gold headdresses
> Met her with joy, draped her in sacred clothes,
> And crowned her deathless head with intricate gold;
> And in her ears, already pierced, went earrings:
> Flowers of precious gold and mountain-copper.
> They hung her tender neck and silvery breasts
> With necklaces of gold, just like the Hours wear
> Themselves when in gold diadems they visit
> Their Father's house to join enticing dances.
> Once they had thoroughly adorned her body,
> They took her to the gods, who made her welcome,
> Each with a hand clasp, each with prayers to take her
> Home as his lawful wife: they were amazed
> By the beauty of the violet-crowned Cytherean.
>
> (hymn 6.5–18, trans. Ruden, 2005)

Like Anchises in hymn 5, the gods mentioned at the end of hymn 6 are all impressed with Aphrodite's beauty and adornment and immediately desire to possess her. Both hymns offer catalog-like descriptions that highlight Aphrodite's beautiful clothing and jewelry, and both passages focus on the bright radiance emanating from the well-adorned goddess. Readers of archaic Greek poetry will recognize such luminosity as a traditional literary motif in scenes of divine epiphany, and shiny brilliance is a familiar quality of beautiful individuals throughout Greek myth and literature. In the hymns, Aphrodite's glow originates from her immortal beauty amplified by a veritable treasure chest of metallic ornaments, mostly made of gold. Indeed, these narrative descriptions of a sumptuously accessorized Aphrodite may correspond to the way the goddess was actually visualized by the ancients. In Greek art, both in vase painting and sculpture, as well as in coin portraits, Aphrodite is frequently represented wearing an abundance of jewelry: earrings, necklaces, bracelets, and a variety of different headbands (for examples of the goddess' adornment depicted in Greek art: Faulkner 2008; Karageorghis 2005). Some scholars also note that literary descriptions of Aphrodite's adornment may suggest parallels to the kosmēsis of cult images, citing numerous inscriptions from the Archaic period onwards that record the costs of material and labor involved in the decoration of cult statues with colorful paint or gold leaf, bright fabrics, gilded crowns and various items of jewelry (most recently, with thorough summary of evidence:

Breitenberger 2007). So the adornment of Aphrodite, as described in the hymns, would be a physical manifestation of her sacred meaning that is intended to demonstrate her divine powers and define her realm of beauty and seduction.

In addition to the two hymns, the motif of Aphrodite's *kosmēsis* also occurs briefly in book 8 of the *Odyssey*, in the song of the bard Demodocus (8.266–369). After her erotic tryst with Ares is discovered by her husband, Hephaestus, and witnessed by the other male Olympians, Aphrodite retreats to her favorite island sanctuary for a soothing spa treatment to renew her beauty and energy.

> And Aphrodite, who loves laughter and smiles,
> To Paphos on Cyprus [went], and her precinct there
> With its smoking altar. There the Graces
> Bathed her and rubbed her with the ambrosial oil
> That glistens on the skin of the immortal gods.
> And then they dressed her in beautiful clothes,
> A wonder to see.

(Odyssey 8.362–66, trans. Lombardo, 2000)

The *Odyssey* passage closely recalls the first hymn 5 passage discussed above in that both passages portray the goddess going to her shrine at Paphos, busy with fragrant offerings, and both cast the *Charites*, or Graces, as her attendants. In each passage, the narrative emphasis is on the bathing scene with its three corresponding features: washing (*lousan*, hymn 5.61; *Odyssey* 8.364); anointing with oil (*chrisan elaiōi ambrotōi*, hymn 5.61–62; *Odyssey* 8.364–65); and donning fresh clothing (*heimata kala*, "fine clothes," hymn 5.64; *heimata epērata*, "lovely clothes," *Odyssey* 8.366). Echoes in outline and phrasing evinced in these two passages may denote a common epic model for the depiction of Aphrodite at her bath, while scholars have also noted that bathing itself is a regular "type scene" in epic (Faulkner 2008); the textual similarities may also indicate that the description of Aphrodite refreshing herself in her Cyprian sanctuary was a conventional motif in epic poetry. Moreover, just as literary accounts of Aphrodite's *kosmēsis* may reflect how the goddess was represented in cult images, the bathing, anointing and dressing episodes may allude to actual cult rituals practiced at festivals celebrating the goddess in the Archaic and later periods (Breitenberger 2007). But thematically, the two passages reveal rather different circumstances: instead of preparing the goddess for a seduction as in the hymn, the bathing scene in the *Odyssey* follows Aphrodite's sexual encounter with her lover. Yet both episodes take place in undeniably erotic contexts, and thereby function as expressions of Aphrodite's power as a divinity of love and attraction.

As a recurrent image that exemplifies Aphrodite's divine activity of erotic pursuit and conquest, scholars have observed how the *kosmēsis* or "adornment scene" evokes thematic and narrative resonances to conventional epic descriptions of warriors arming themselves for battle; for instance, Achilles prepares himself for his *aristeia* in the final combat spree in book 19 of the *Iliad* (19.364–91) (Podbielski 1971; Clay 1989; Smith 1981). Other scholars argue that the *kosmēsis* scene as a motif has conspicuous parallels in Near Eastern literature, suggesting that the mythological discourse regarding the Greek Aphrodite may have been influenced early on by the transmission of cultural material from the East (most recently, with overview of evidence: Faulkner 2008; Budin 2003; West 1997). For example, Near Eastern mythological narratives describe how the Sumerian love goddess Inanna bathes, anoints herself with oil, and covers her body with jewelry before she seduces the mortal shepherd, Dumuzi. In the Near Eastern text of the *Descent of Ishtar to the Netherworld*, the love goddess Ishtar dons clothing and jewelry, removes each item as she descends into the lower world, and then reclaims them piece by piece as she returns back to the world of the living. So it is fair to say that scenes of Aphrodite's adornment, along with the epiphanies that often accompany them, have several intermingled functions and meanings. On the narrative level, *kosmēsis* scenes prepare the goddess for a successful seduction, as in the case of the mortal cattleman Anchises in the fifth Homeric hymn, and the group of gods who desire her in the sixth Homeric hymn; or in the song of Demodocus in the *Odyssey*, the *kosmēsis* happens after her erotic tryst with her lover, Ares. Most importantly, adornment scenes demarcate and establish the goddess' particular province of erotic attraction, while vividly exhibiting her divine power to mingle the ideas of love, beauty, embellishment and sexual allure.

Garlands and mirrors

In addition to fine clothing and glittering jewelry, Aphrodite, the goddess of "beauty enhanced for a purpose," is closely associated with many other attributes and articles that are part of her personal adornment, such as garlands, flowers, fruits, perfume and incense. What these objects have in common are their appealing qualities of color, taste, fragrance, charm, sweetness, and the synaesthetic pleasures derived from adorning the head and body with these sense-gratifying items. As

Figure 4.1 Aphrodite with mirror. Red-figure vase, Sicilian, *ca.* fourth century BC. The Art Archive/Archaeological Museum Syracuse/Gianni Dagli Orti.

tangible emblems of her divine power to augment beauty and allure, Aphrodite's traditional floral and aromatic attributes function as multi-sensory symbols of the methods and means used to attract sexual part-ners. In a fragment of a lost epic poem called the *Cypria*, which told of the events leading up to the Trojan War and was probably composed in the seventh or sixth century BC, the poet describes the *kosmēsis* of Aphrodite with a particular focus on the flowery nature of her adornment.

She clothed herself in garments which the Graces and Hours had made for her and dyed in flowers of spring – such flowers as the Hours wear – in crocus and hyacinth and flourishing violet and the rose's lovely bloom, so sweet and delicious, and heavenly buds, the flowers of the narcissus and lily. In such perfumed garments is Aphrodite clothed at all seasons.

Then laughter-loving Aphrodite and her handmaidens wove sweet-smelling crowns of flowers of the earth and put them upon their heads – the bright coiffed goddesses, the Nymphs and Graces, and golden Aphrodite too, while they sang sweetly on the mount of many-fountained Ida.

(*Cypria* fragment 6.1–12, trans. Evelyn-White, 1936)

Like the *kosmēsis* descriptions discussed earlier, the poet of the *Cypria* lists a series of beautiful items, producing an almost incantatory, layering effect to underscore the potency of the goddess' vibrant appearance. Among the *Cypria* fragment's inventory of flowers whose aromatic essence is infused into Aphrodite's clothes – crocus, hyacinth, violet, rose, narcissus and lily – are several blooms that reappear in other Greek literary and artistic depictions of the goddess. Readers will note that an abundance of assorted flowers is a conventional feature of an erotic setting in early Greek poetry: for example, in the *Dios Apatē* scene in book 14 of the *Iliad*, Hera and Zeus make love on a bed of dewy blossoms: lotus, crocus and hyacinth (14.346–51); while in the *Homeric Hymn to Demeter*, the goddess' daughter, Persephone, is seized by an amorous Hades as she is playing in a luxuriant field of flowers: hyacinth, violet, iris, crocus, rose and narcissus (hymn 2.5–9). Just as flowers can evoke an erotic literary context, scholars observe that Aphrodite herself is linked to many flowers, and by extension, various fruit (on this dimension of the goddess: Friedrich 1978). As noted above, even some of her jewelry is fashioned in floral shape (*kalukes*, "buds," hymn 5.87; *anthema*, "blooms," hymn 6.9).

In particular, the rose, *rhodon* in Greek, is associated with Aphrodite in the earliest texts: for example, to protect the body of Hector at the end of the *Iliad*, she uses immortal oil of rose (*rhodoenti elaiōi ambrotōi*, 23.185–87); and the archaic poet Ibycus praises a handsome youth by declaring in a verse that Aphrodite nursed him "among rose blossoms" (*rhodeoisin en anthesi*, fragment 288.4). The ancient Greek travel writer Pausanias confirms the rose and the myrtle tree are sacred to Aphrodite, as they are both linked to the story of her mortal lover Adonis (*Description of Greece* 6.24.7). Other flowers sometimes linked to Aphrodite are the lily and poppy, the latter perhaps for its narcotic effects which evoke the enchantment of sexual desire. One of Aphrodite's fruits is said to be the pomegranate, perhaps because its numerous red seeds suggest sexuality and procreation: in the *Homeric Hymn to Demeter*, when Persephone eats pomegranate seeds in the Underworld, it is a symbol of her irreversible acquisition of sexual knowledge (hymn 2.411–13). In ancient times, women evidently used pomegranate (as well as penny-royal mint) as birth-control medications to prevent fertility and even as abortifacients: this may suggest a link to Aphrodite's influence over non-maternal sexuality, since Persephone bears no children (Rayor 2004). But Aphrodite's most important fruit is the apple, the emblem of her victory in the mythological beauty contest after the Judgment of Paris, a trophy which bore the inscription "to the most beautiful." In ancient Greek society, the apple becomes the love token par excellence.

A natural outgrowth of Aphrodite's association to flowers is her iconographical link to floral crowns, or garlands. The *Cypria* fragment describes how Aphrodite and her entourage weave flowers into "sweet-smelling garlands" (*stephanous euōdeas*, 9); and indeed, several literary epithets using the word *stephanos*, "garland," indicate Aphrodite's close relation to the colorful, aromatic wreaths (Boedeker 1974). While some scholars interpret this as an example of Aphrodite's association with fertility, it is also likely to be an expression of her image as a goddess of beauty and adornment who wears garlands for their ability to enhance attractiveness with fragrance and color. Aphrodite is often called *eustephanos*, "well garlanded," an epithet that usually occurs at verse end in early Greek poetry with the title Cythereia, *eustephanos Cythereia* (*Odyssey* 8.288, 18.193; *Theogony* 196, 1008; *Homeric Hymn to Aphrodite*: hymn 5.6, 175, 287), while the epic epithet *eustophanos* describes Aphrodite by name only once, as the bard Demodocus begins his song (*Odyssey* 8.267). Aphrodite shares the epithet *eustephanos* with other female figures, in particular the goddess Demeter in the *Homeric Hymn to Demeter* (hymn 2.224, 307, 384, 470; also *Works and Days* 300). Two *stephanos* compounds occur only once as epithets of Aphrodite in Greek poetry: *philostephanos* "loving garlands" (in the *Homeric Hymn to Demeter*: hymn 2.102); and *iostephanos* "violet garlanded" with the title Cythereia (*Homeric Hymn to Aphrodite*: hymn 6.18). Aphrodite's literary epithets indicating her connection to garlands correspond to her universal association with flowers, and both complement the visualized persona of the goddess of ornamentation.

A key feature of flowers and garlands is, of course, their sweet smell, and scholars have noted that fragrance, both of incense and perfume, plays an important role in the literature, mythology and cult of Aphrodite (most recently, with extensive survey of evidence: Pirenne-Delforge 1994). In early Greek poetry, the sensation of an appealing aroma regularly denotes a divine dwelling-place, such as Mt. Olympus, which is often called "fragrant" *thuōdēs* (hymn 2.331; hymn 4.322); sweet scent may also imply the presence of an erotically beautiful woman, for example, Helen's bedchamber is called "fragrant" *thuōdēs* (*Odyssey* 4.121), and the nymph Calypso bathes her lover, Odysseus, and gives him "fragrant clothing" *heimata thuōdea* (*Odyssey* 5.264). For Aphrodite, fragrance is suggestive of both the divine and erotic contexts, with a blurring of the two boundaries that the goddess of *mixis* uniquely inspires. The poet of the fifth Homeric hymn repeatedly emphasizes the property of fragrance in his description of Aphrodite's *kosmēsis* before her seduction of Anchises (Faulkner 2008): her temple, precinct and altar at Paphos are all "fragrant" *thuōdēs* (hymn 5.58–59); the immortal oil the Graces rub over her body is "perfumed" *tethuōmenon* (63); and after Aphrodite completes her adornment, the entire island gives off an exquisite scent, *euōdea Kupron* (66). Aphrodite's clothes in the *Cypria* fragment are imbued with floral aroma (*tethuōmena heimata*, 7). In a fragment of a kletic hymn, Sappho summons Aphrodite to her temple on the island of Crete, and describes the setting in a sacred grove of apple trees, blooming with roses and spring flowers, where the altars are smoky with sweet-smelling "frankincense" *libanōtos* (fragment 2.4). According to some scholars, in the later Hellenistic Greek period, Aphrodite is also associated with the more specific botanical scents of myrrh, cinnamon, clove, cassia and fennel (on the link between perfume and the myth of Aphrodite and Adonis: Detienne 1972). Fragrance is an essential component of the goddess' divinity, beauty and allure.

Not surprisingly, Aphrodite is associated in later Greek poetry and art with mirrors. As a symbol of the goddess, the mirror encapsulates the powerful moment of epiphany and recognition when the beautiful appearance of Aphrodite is perceived by someone else, as Anchises first sees her in the fifth Homeric hymn (hymn 5.84–90): in that instant of perception, the divinity of the goddess is made manifest. In later Greek art, the mirror becomes one of the most important and conventional symbols of Aphrodite as the goddess of beauty and adornment. A Paestan red-figure kalyx krater, attributed to the painter Python (dated to *ca.* 360–340 BC), depicts a well-dressed Aphrodite lavishly decked out with jewelry – earrings, necklaces, bracelets and jeweled headband – with one hand saucily on her hip and the other holding a mirror, as she admires her stunning visage. The mirror becomes such an established emblem of the goddess that when the Aphrodite of Arles, a life-size marble statue probably dating to the late Hellenistic period (Havelock 1995), was discovered near a Roman theater in 1651, the French sculptor who restored her arms placed a mirror in one hand, and an apple in the other.

In earlier Greek times, Aphrodite may have been linked with mirrors because they were made of bronze, a metal alloy consisting primarily of copper with some other metal additive (usually tin), and copper was associated with Aphrodite because of its abundance on the island of Cyprus. Perhaps the rosy metallic shine of copper also evoked the radiance of the jewelry-bedecked goddess. The sign known as the "Venus mirror," a cross beneath a circle, which in biology signifies the female gender and in astronomy signifies the planet Venus, is the periodic-table symbol for the chemical element copper: the English word "copper" is related to the Latin *cuprum*, "metal from Cyprus." A number of bronze mirrors that survive from antiquity, and in particular from the fourth century BC, are engraved with depictions of Aphrodite, as the goddess of beautification, alone or with other figures such as Eros or Pan, as well as with erotic or *toilette* scenes. Mirrors were often dedicated in temples and sanctuaries of Aphrodite, sometimes by courtesans: for example, an epigram by Philetas of Cos (*ca.* late fourth century BC) records that the retiring courtesan Nikias dedicated, along with her sandals and a long lock of hair, "the bronze mirror that never lied to her" (poem 88, *Greek Anthology* 6.210, trans. Rexroth, 1999). Another example of such a dedication of feminine *accoutrement* is commemorated in this epigram by the poet Leonidas of Tarentum (*ca.* third century BC).

A silver Love, an anklet,
Purple curls of her Lesbian
Hair, her translucent brassiere,
Her bronze mirror, the broad comb
Of boxwood that restrained her
Ringlets, Kallikleia hangs up
In the porch of faithful Kypris,
In thanks for her granted wish.

(poem 46, *Greek Anthology* 6.211, trans. Rexroth, 1999)

Aphrodite's iconographical association with *kosmēsis*, specifically of her hair and head, together with her emblematic link to garlands and crowns, may also be connected to the hair-grooming scenes that are ubiquitous in later Greek poetry and art. In book 3 of the *Argonautica*, the tale of Jason's quest for the Golden Fleece, written by Apollonius of Rhodes at Alexandria in the third century BC, Aphrodite is shown gracefully grooming her hair when Hera and Athena come seeking her aid.

> She [Aphrodite] had let down her hair on to her two white shoulders and was grooming it through with a golden comb, preparatory to plaiting the long tresses. When she saw the goddesses in front of her she stopped and called them in, and rising from her chair, sat them down on couches. Then she too sat down again, and put up her hair without finishing the combing. She smiled as she addressed them with flattering deference.
>
> (*Argonautica* 3.45–51, trans. Hunter, 1993)

Scholars note that the literary image of Aphrodite grooming her hair may be indebted to artistic portrayals of the goddess (Hunter 1989). The depiction of Aphrodite dressing, washing or wringing out her hair becomes more frequent in Greek art starting in the late fourth century BC, and reaches a peak of artistic popularity in the statues of Aphrodite *Anadyomenē*, "Rising from the Sea," dating from the late Hellenistic period (Havelock 1995). For example, in the crouching *Anadyomenē* type, such as the lovely Aphrodite of Rhodes, the kneeling, nude goddess reaches up with both hands to hold out her long, curly locks on either side of her head. Other *Anadyomenē* figures, both semi-draped and nude types, show Aphrodite with both arms raised to her long hair, which she appears to be twisting into thick, rope-like tresses, either to squeeze water from or plait them. The activity of hair grooming depicted in the Aphrodite *Anadyomenē* statues is clearly related to the Hesiodic birth myth of the goddess' emergence from the foamy waters of the sea (*Theogony* 188–206), while at the same time such images evoke her specific association with *kosmēsis* and beautification. As we have seen in the epigrams above, both hair combs and locks of hair are attested as appropriate dedications at temples and shrines of Aphrodite, goddess of beauty and adornment.

Goldenness

A crucial feature of Aphrodite's luminous beauty is the property of "goldenness." In ancient Greek poetry, Aphrodite is distinctively described as *chruseē*, "golden," and the quality of "goldenness" is her intrinsic and eternal characteristic. Many Greek deities, both gods and goddesses, are said to possess golden objects and attributes; and so they are often depicted by compound epithets made up of *chrus*- "golden" joined with another element: for example, golden-sandaled, golden-throned, golden-sceptered, and golden-bowed. But only Aphrodite is herself inherently "golden": in fact, the adjective *chruseē* "golden" is her most frequent descriptive epithet (Boedeker 1974; Friedrich 1978).

Figure 4.2 Aphrodite of Rhodes. Hellenistic Greek marble, *ca.* second century BC. The Art Archive/Archaeological Museum Rhodes/Gianni Dagli Orti.

For the ancient Greek poets, gold is the most exalted, beautiful and high-status metal. In the *Iliad*, gold is the principal metal used by the blacksmith god, Hephaestus, to forge the new shield of Achilles (18.462–617); several scenes on the shield are engraved in gold, such as the plowmen working in the fields: "It was gold, all gold, forged to a wonder" (*Iliad* 18.549, trans. Lombardo, 1997). The poet Pindar (*ca.* 518–438 BC), who composed long victory odes in commemoration of winning athletes, begins his tribute to the Olympic victor Hieron, tyrant of Syracuse,

by declaring that "gold, like blazing fire by night, shines forth pre-
eminent amid the lordliness of wealth" (*Olympian* 1.1–2, trans. Miller,
1996). So to compare something to gold or describe it as "golden" is to
mark it with the prestige of immortality, superiority, affluence and
beauty, all traits that inform Aphrodite's image as "the golden one." In an
elegiac verse by the Ionian Greek poet Mimnermus, composed in the late
seventh century BC, the "goldenness" of Aphrodite encapsulates the
foremost erotic aspects of her divinity.

> What life, what pleasure is there without golden Aphrodite?
> May I die when I no longer care about such things
> as clandestine love and cajoling gifts and bed,
> which are the alluring blossoms of youth
> for men and women.
>
> (fragment 1.1–5, trans. Miller, 1996)

The epithet *chruseē* "golden" occurs regularly in the early texts joined
with the name Aphrodite, and almost always occupies the verse-ending
position, except for one instance where the variant adjective *chruseiē*
is used midline: this occurs when Achilles says he would not marry
Agamemnon's daughter even if she "rivaled golden Aphrodite in beauty"
(*Iliad* 9.390). As an epithet used distinctively of her, the phrase "golden
Aphrodite" appears numerous times in the Homeric epics (*Iliad* 3.64,
5.427, 9.390, 19.282, 22.470; *Odyssey* 4.14, 8.337, 342, 17.37, 19.54), and
the narrative poems of Hesiod (*Theogony* 822, 962, 975, 1005, 1014;
Works and Days 65); and once in the fifth Homeric hymn (hymn 5.93).
Scholars have observed that the epithet *chruseē* is more than merely
superficial, and may relate to Aphrodite's earliest mythological functions
and meaning as a goddess of beauty and adornment (Boedeker 1974).
The phrase "golden Aphrodite" seems to be used in contexts where
Aphrodite's exceptional beauty is being emphasized, as in the several
examples cited above where poets praise a mortal woman's appearance
by comparing her to the goddess: for example, Hermione, the daughter
of Helen, "had the looks of golden Aphrodite" (*Odyssey* 4.14). The epithet
also occurs in situations where the goddess herself supplies adornment,
such as when Zeus bids "golden Aphrodite" to beautify the first woman,
Pandora (*Works and Days* 65); also, the headdress of Andromache, wife
of Hector, is a wedding gift from "golden Aphrodite" (*Iliad* 22.470). But
the auric symbolism evident in the epithet *chruseē* is most directly
evocative of Aphrodite's own shiny *kosmēsis*, with her multiple layers of
glistening gold jewelry, especially as described in the two Homeric
hymns (see above: hymn 5.84–90; hymn 6.5–18). After readying herself to

seduce Anchises, Aphrodite emerges "adorned with gold" *chrusōi kosmētheisa* (hymn 5.65). Some scholars detect a correspondence between Aphrodite's link to gold jewelry and the depiction in art and literature of the elaborate jewelry of Near Eastern love goddesses (Faulkner 2008; Karageorghis 2005); while others note that Aphrodite's epithet *chrusee* "golden" may reflect the artistic representation of her cult statues and figurines, decorated with gold leaf, gold paint and gold jewelry (Breitenberger 2007). As a value signifier, ornamentation made of gold metal indicates divinity, beauty and status.

Aphrodite's association with gold also suggests the visual properties of light. Descriptions of Aphrodite's beauty and adornment, as we have seen earlier, typically include the phenomenon of luminosity: the poets describe her bright eyes, shimmering clothes and glittering jewels. Radiance is a traditional literary motif in portrayals of divine epiphany, and in Greek narratives when gods reveal themselves to humans, they are often surrounded by dazzling light. Yet the textual emphasis on the brilliant shine of Aphrodite's physical appearance and *kosmēsis* implies a deeper connection to her distinctive epithet *chrusee* "golden," one that may be related to her celestial aspect as *Ourania*, the "Heavenly" goddess. In an interesting visual contrast of shiny metals, the archaic Greek poet Pindar (522–443 BC) describes Aphrodite as having "silvery feet," *arguropeza* (*Pythian* 9.9).

Two epithets compounded with *chrus-*"golden" attached to Aphrodite may further illuminate the significance of gold in her mythological persona. In the first line of the sixth Homeric hymn, Aphrodite is referred to as *chrusostephanos*, "gold-crowned" (hymn 6.1; also, Sappho fragment 9.1), an epithet that joins two of her significant attributes, garlands and gold. When Aphrodite comes ashore on Cyprus, the Hours, wearing "gold headdresses," *chrusampukes* (hymn 6.5, 12), adorn Aphrodite with a profusion of gold jewelry and place upon her head a "crown of gold," *stephanēn chruseiēn* (hymn 6.7–8). Whether the crown is purely decorative or an indication of the goddess' sovereignty, or both, is unclear: recent scholarship suggests Aphrodite was worshipped at Paphos as *Wanassa*, or "Queen" (Budin 2003). Aphrodite is also called *polychrusos*, "very, intensely golden," a few times in early Greek poetry (e.g. hymn 5.1, 9; *Works and Days* 521; *Theogony* 980). In the Homeric epics, the epithet *polychrusos* is never joined to Aphrodite but is used to characterize cities or men as "having much gold, wealthy": for example, rich Mycenae (*Iliad* 7.180, 11.46; *Odyssey* 3.304); affluent Troy (*Iliad* 18.289); and the greedy Trojan, Dolon (*Iliad* 10.315). The Attic tragedian, Aeschylus, employs the adjective *polychrusos* several times to describe the fabulously wealthy Persians in the opening of his earliest extant play (*Persians* 3, 5, 45, 53), where the word perhaps also alludes to oriental extravagance (Faulkner 2008). As an epithet used to portray Aphrodite, *polychrusos* may also hint at her association with prostitution, and the affluence of the working girls under her protection. Thus, the term *polychrusos* "very golden" describing Aphrodite not only provides an expansion on *chruseē* "golden" appropriate to the image of the goddess, but the compound epithet also conveys an added sense of material wealth, luxury and prestige.

Entourage

Aphrodite is attended by groups of specifically named minor goddesses who are charged with maintaining her beauty, clothing and adornment, and thus often appear in her *kosmēsis* scenes. The most important and ubiquitous members of Aphrodite's "beauty team" are the *Charites*, or Graces, who appear frequently in Greek art, literature and mythology as the attendants of Aphrodite, primarily at her *toilette* (most recently, with thorough review of scholarship: MacLachlan 1993; see also Larson 2001). In the works of the Greek poets and artists, the Graces are imagined as lithe, gorgeous young women who personify the idea of *charis*, the Greek word for "beauty, grace, loveliness," an external quality with explicitly erotic connotations: namely, *charis* imparts an alluring, attractive beauty that captivates and invites *mixis*, "sexual mingling." Since Aphrodite embodies this erotic "charisma" – the word is derived from *charis* – the Graces share an affinity with the goddess of love and beauty both as personified aspects of her divine sphere as well as her most intimate companions. In the earliest Greek texts, as we have seen, the Graces attend Aphrodite at her favorite shrine on the island of Cyprus, where they bathe the goddess, anoint her with oil and dress her in new clothing, both after she makes love to Ares (*Odyssey* 8.364–66), and before she seduces Anchises (hymn 5.61–65). The Graces also see to Aphrodite's clothing: they weave her dress (*Iliad* 5.338), and dye her garments in spring colors (*Cypria* fragment 6.1–2). Sometimes the Graces join Aphrodite to beautify others, as in Hesiod's story of the first mortal woman, Pandora: after Zeus bids Aphrodite "to pour *charis* on her head" (*Works and Days* 65), the Graces adorn her with "golden necklaces" (73). In this remarkable passage, Hesiod merges the abstract notion of *charis*, "beauty, grace," with the Graces as personified agents of beautification. Like Aphrodite, the Graces are associated with flowers and garlands, as in this poetic fragment, where Sappho urges a friend to propitiate them with floral adornment.

Place lovely garlands, Dika, around your hair,

twining together shoots of dill with your tender hands;

for the blessed Graces too prefer things decked with flowers

to gaze upon, and turn aside from those that are ungarlanded.

(fragment 81.1–4, trans. Miller, 1996)

While the number and genealogy of the Graces varies with different authors and time periods, Hesiod's version is traditionally accepted: he says the Graces are the three daughters of Zeus and Eurynome, an Oceanid, and names them as *Aglaea*, "Splendor," *Euphrosyne*, "Good Cheer," and *Thalia*, "Abundance"; he also describes the intense erotic power emanating from their "glancing eyes" (*Theogony* 907–11). Scholars cite evidence that the Graces were worshipped from very ancient times and enjoyed their own cults in archaic Greece or even earlier, and originally may have been identified with nymphs as nature deities (most recently, with survey of evidence: Breitenberger 2007). At some point the Graces became associated with Aphrodite, and traces of this early intersection can still be found in the Homeric epics. In the *Iliad*, the wife of Hephaestus is called Charis, who receives the sea goddess Thetis into their home (*Iliad* 18.382: note how the blacksmith god lists all the pieces of jewelry he fashioned for Thetis, 18.401); but in the *Odyssey*, as we have seen in the song of Demodocus episode, his wife is the adulterous Aphrodite (*Odyssey* 8.266–369). Hesiod says Aglaea, whom he calls "the youngest of the Graces," is the wife of Hephaestus (*Theogony* 945). It is uncertain whether this mythological interchange in the early texts reflects the actual process by which the Graces were assimilated with Aphrodite; but we have noted how other personified aspects of Aphrodite's divine province, such as Peithō, Eros and Himeros, become subordinated to the goddess as her assistants or companions. Although the Graces are most closely linked to Aphrodite as personifications of physical beauty, they are also associated with poetry, dancing, festivals and athletic victory; while the abstract concept of *charis* itself is also used to express the ideas of "kindness, favor, gratitude."

The other significant members of Aphrodite's beauty entourage are the *Horae*, or Hours: their collective name is also sometimes translated as the Seasons. The word *hōra* in Greek denotes a fixed period of time, whether of the year, month or day, and can refer in particular to the prime or peak portion of that time; thus *hōra* can signify the leading season of springtime. This linguistic link is borne out by the mythical personification of the Horae, who are specifically associated with spring, and said to wear "spring flowers" (*Cypria* fragment 6.2–3). Hesiod supplies the names and genealogy of the Hours: they are the daughters of

Zeus and the Titaness, Themis, and their names are *Eunomia*, "Good Order," *Dikē*, "Justice," and *Eirēnē*, "Peace" (*Theogony* 901–2). The Hours regularly accompany the Graces as attendants of Aphrodite, and sometimes they attend the goddess alone. Like the Graces, the Hours welcome Aphrodite on the beach at Cyprus, adorn her with dresses, jewelry and a golden crown, then escort her to join the gods (hymn 6.5–18); together with the Graces, the Hours dye Aphrodite's clothing "in spring flowers" (*Cypria* fragment 6.1–2). The Hours also assist Aphrodite in the beautification of Pandora, whom they crown "with spring flowers" (*Works and Days* 74–75). In the *Homeric Hymn to Apollo*, composed in the seventh or sixth century BC, the poet describes an extraordinary scene on Mt. Olympus, where Apollo plays the lyre, the Muses sing, and Aphrodite joins the dance with her beloved companions.

> The smooth-haired Graces and the cheerful Hours,
> Zeus' child Aphrodite, Harmony,
> And Youth dance there, hands on each other's wrists.
>
> (hymn 3.194–96, trans. Ruden, 2005)

Two other minor goddesses are present on the dancing floor, both personifications who are allied to Aphrodite as the goddess of love and beauty: *Harmonia*, "Harmony," Aphrodite's daughter by Ares (*Theogony* 934–37), and *Hēbē*, "Youth," the daughter of Zeus and Hera (*Theogony* 921–23). Linked together like a garland, the image of the dancers exemplifies the network of intermingled attributes and concepts that establish Aphrodite's divine function and meaning. The Graces and Hours, two sets of Aphrodite's chief attendants, complement each other as they cultivate and supply the tangible emblems of Aphrodite's sphere of authority: clothing, jewelry, crowns, cosmetics, perfume and flowers. This impressive immortal entourage is a conspicuous sign of Aphrodite's universal power.

NUDITY

The nudity of Aphrodite, as portrayed in Greek art, literature and cult, is an expression of her eternal power, autonomy and meaning. Indeed, the main iconographic purpose of her external ornamentation is to define and emphasize her perfect, immortal nakedness. As the divine embodiment of feminine beauty, we have seen how the goddess herself is inseparable from the idea of physical adornment with the goal of allure and seduction. Descriptions of Aphrodite's *kosmēsis* to enhance sexual

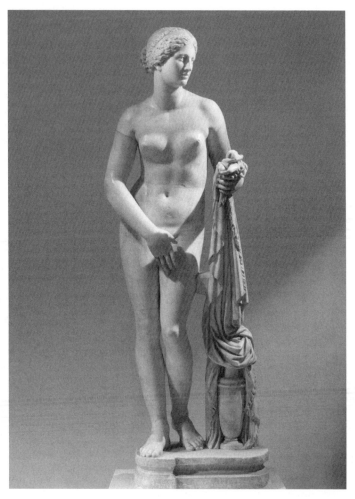

Figure 4.3 Aphrodite of Knidos. Roman copy after Praxiteles, ca. 350 BC. The Art Archive/Museo Nazionale Palazzo Altemps Rome/Gianni Dagli Orti.

attractiveness, along with scenes of her dressing and undressing in general, are highly charged with erotic excitement and expectation, since they often precede or follow sexual activity. Such scenes also draw attention to the goddess' corporeal beauty and thus are intimately related to the trope of Aphrodite's nakedness. Literary depictions of Aphrodite's beauty and adornment tend to accentuate and extol the contours of her body, which is always clearly identifiable beneath the profusion of flowers, gold jewelry and ambrosial oils. In these descriptive passages, there is often a particular emphasis on the goddess' beautiful breasts: Helen recognizes Aphrodite in disguise by the distinctive splendor of her "lovely breasts," *stēthea himeroenta* (*Iliad* 3.397); Anchises is stunned by the glow, which he correctly assumes is divine, emanating from her "tender breasts," *stēthesin hapaloisin* (hymn 5.90); and the Hours adorn the goddess with gold necklaces to highlight the swell of her "silvery breasts," *stēthesin argupheoisin* (hymn 6.10–11). Rather than offering any concealment, the embellishment of the goddess draws attention to her signature feature, as if her beautiful breasts were bare to the gaze of the viewer. In the song of Demodocus, the male gods gather and cheerfully savor the exposure of Aphrodite's naked body as she is caught in a trap set by her cuckolded husband, Hephaestus (*Odyssey* 8.321–43). While the bard notes that the other female deities avoid the titillating spectacle out of "modesty," *aidoi* (8.324), Aphrodite blithely accepts the attention, and then decamps to her shrine at Paphos to bathe and refresh her recently exposed body (8.362–66). Unlike Artemis or Athena, whose myths underscore the punishments of those who behold their nakedness, Aphrodite is never shamed, vengeful or diminished by the revelation of her nude body in the Greek texts. Aphrodite's nudity is as intrinsic to her divinity as her goldenness, beauty and sexuality.

The motif of nakedness in the iconography of Aphrodite finds expression in ancient Greek art as well, but many questions remain as to when, where and how nudity becomes a discernible physical attribute of the goddess. Scholars continue to speculate about widespread and abundant archaeological evidence suggesting a so-called "Nude Goddess" archetype existed starting from the late Bronze Age (*ca.* 1100 BC) throughout the Mediterranean area in numerous representations: for example, Minoan, Cycladic and Mycenaean Greek types (Böhm 1990); Syrian and Phoenician-influenced Cypriot versions (Budin 2003); and Near Eastern varieties (Moorey 2004). The "Nude Goddess" is typically a naked female figure standing rigidly upright and facing forward; her arms are upraised, often holding flowers or other objects, or cupping a breast with one hand; the figure's rounded breasts and genital triangle are regularly emphasized; the figure is often shown wearing jewelry, such as necklaces, bracelets and anklets; and sometimes she is accompanied by birds or lions. Whether any of these ancient images can be associated with or identified as Aphrodite is, not surprisingly, the source of much debate: some scholars automatically identify any nude figure as the Greek goddess of sex, while others justifiably argue that just because a female figure is naked does not necessarily indicate she must be Aphrodite. Yet the "Nude Goddess" type did have an unmistakable influence on early

Greek art: starting in the ninth and eighth centuries BC, the image was repeatedly reproduced in both decorative and religious contexts, especially in the minor arts, such as clay plaques, bronze mirrors and metallic jewelry. Scholars note that from the eighth to the sixth centuries BC, small terracotta figurines showing a fully naked female figure were in wide distribution in the eastern Mediterranean (Havelock 1995), but the image of the "Nude Goddess" appears to become much less popular after the sixth century BC. Since Greek artists did not portray their major female deities in the nude during this period, it is unlikely that these figurines represent the goddess Aphrodite, or any other Greek goddess for that matter. Rather, the naked images may simply respond to an artistic trend during the Archaic period for creating exotic, "oriental"-style female figures. Indeed, it would take the passing of a couple more centuries, and the transition to a different cultural, social and artistic milieu, for the first Greek goddess to be depicted fully nude. She was, of course, Aphrodite, the embodiment of divine female beauty.

The Knídia

The first statue of the naked Aphrodite in three-dimensional and monumental form was conceived and sculpted by the late classical artist Praxiteles of Athens (*ca.* 400–340 BC). As the first sculpture of a life-size female nude, Praxiteles' work was more than just an innovation: his Aphrodite represented a revolution in the history of art (most recently, with comprehensive survey of evidence and exceptional collection of plates: Havelock 1995). The statue, carved in Parian marble, was purchased by the city of Knidos (in southwest Turkey) in around 350 BC. The *Knidia*, as the statue was known, was displayed as a cult image in the sanctuary of Aphrodite *Euploia*, "She of the Smooth Sailing," at the end of a narrow peninsula facing the sea and the busy shipping lanes over which the goddess of seafaring had jurisdiction. According to the romantic accounts of ancient authors, Praxiteles used his mistress Phryne, a celebrated and extremely beautiful Greek courtesan, as the model for his statue of Aphrodite. One particularly sexy anecdote describes how the enchanting Phryne disrobed and loosened her hair on the beach at Eleusis, then walked naked and resplendent into the sea: we are told Praxiteles immediately fell in love with her and decided to model his Aphrodite on her gorgeous nudity (recorded *ca.* AD 200 by Athenaeus 13.590). Even if sensationalized (and late), the story of a passionate liaison between the great artist and his proud model would have added a *frisson* of erotic excitement to a viewing of the statue. The Aphrodite of

Knidos, initially cherished as a cult image and a famous work of art, was soon to become a major tourist attraction in antiquity, drawing scores of Greek and Roman sightseers to her shrine to behold her ideal feminine beauty.

Although Praxiteles' Aphrodite does not survive, a great many copies of the statue, in various sizes and different media, have been found all over the Mediterranean world, demonstrating the immense popularity of the image during ancient times. Based on this evidence, scholars can offer a tentative reconstruction of what the original statue may have looked like. The *Knidia* most likely stood in a classic *contrapposto* pose with her weight on one leg while the other is relaxed; her head was turned slightly away from the frontal axis; and her hair was centrally divided and pulled back. The defining gesture of the statue was that she held one hand near her pubic zone, while the other held a piece of drapery over a tall *hydria*, or water vase, next to her feet. As a cult statue, the *Knidia* was probably life-size or a little larger. Some scholars regard the Colonna version of the statue, now in the Vatican Museum in Rome, to be the most reliable replica (Havelock 1995). As a cult image, the Aphrodite of Knidos offers a visual epiphany imbued with religious significance that renders her divine power explicit to the viewer. Her serene nudity is a symbol of her primordial emergence from the sea as told in the Hesiodic birth narrative (*Theogony* 188–206), with the nearby *hydria* also alluding to her aquatic origins. Self-confident, alluring and radiantly beautiful, the nude Aphrodite also expresses her divine influence over the realm of sexuality, as the gesture of her hand over her genitalia invites the viewer to acknowledge her erotic power.

The *Knidia* of Praxiteles had an unsurpassed influence on later Greek sculptural versions of Aphrodite, in particular during the late Hellenistic period (150–100 BC), when the naked figure of the goddess of love emerged as an exceptionally popular subject in Greek art. Scholars have cataloged several thematic variations among these nude, and some would say increasingly sensuous, statue types inspired by the *Knidia* (Havelock 1995). These include the *Anadyomenē* figures mentioned above, both crouching and standing versions, where the nude goddess is depicted as "rising from the sea" and lifting her hands to squeeze water from her tresses: like the *Knidia*, these figures also make unambiguous reference to Aphrodite's marine birth. Another type is the Aphrodite *Kallipygos* "Beautiful Buttocks," where the goddess' bare backside is prominently displayed to the viewer. Greek sculptural variations such as these were adopted, copied and collected by the Romans, who oversaw the widespread circulation of numerous Aphrodite statue types, for both ornamental and religious purposes, throughout the Mediterranean

world; while at the same time, small-scale marble and clay versions
found their way into private homes and workshops across the empire.
Thanks to the genius of Praxiteles, more statues and representations
of the nude Aphrodite survive from antiquity than of any other Greek
divinity.

OVERVIEW

Aphrodite's beauty and ornamentation form an integral part of her
divine nature. In this chapter, we have seen how Aphrodite's link to the
process of beautification is intimately connected to her role as the goddess of erotic allure, as the obvious purpose of physical adornment is to
boost sexual charm to attract potential lovers. The goddess is especially
associated with flowers, garlands, cosmetics and fragrance, and she is
designated by the epithet "golden," reflecting her connection to gold
ornaments and jewelry, as well as her inherent celestial goldenness.
Aphrodite's illustrious entourage of minor goddesses and personifications complements and enhances her beauty. Ultimately, this plentiful
and rich decoration serves to accentuate Aphrodite's exquisite naked
body, which she displays to express her divine power and autonomy.
The cult image of Praxiteles is the essential revelation of her luminous
immortal nudity for her worshippers and admirers alike.

5

INTIMACY WITH MORTALS

In this chapter, we will look at Aphrodite's intimate relationships and interactions with mortals as recounted in Greek mythology, literature and cult. We will consider several different human and semi-human figures with whom Aphrodite shares noteworthy contact, in close associations that are sometimes beneficial and sometimes detrimental to the mortals in question. We will examine how each individual involvement corresponds in some meaningful way to a specific characteristic of Aphrodite's divinity: above all, her links with mortals reflect her divine influence in the areas of love, sex, war, beauty and adornment. This chapter will also show how Aphrodite's frequent and persistent proximity to the earthly realm functions as an explicit manifestation of her universal power and significance in the imaginations of the ancient Greeks.

INTIMACY

Aphrodite is actively engaged in the human sphere with a few favorite mortals. Indeed, several Greek myths describe Aphrodite's remarkable intimacy with specific individuals upon the terrestrial plane. The familiarity Aphrodite expresses with her human associates exhibits various contours often with very different implications, consequences and outcomes. Aphrodite's demonstration of intimacy with mortals reveals two distinct and conspicuous sides. On the positive side, she can be solicitous and protective towards her mortal friends and favorites; almost affectionate towards her half-human children; and an enthusiastic and appreciative sexual partner with her mortal lovers. On the negative side, she can be demanding and irritable with those who seek to challenge or defy her, and downright cruel and vengeful to those who disrespect her or attempt to disregard her authority. Whether the attention she offers is favoritism or punishment, each of Aphrodite's relationships with a mortal encapsulates and confirms a particular aspect of her overall divinity. Let us review some of the most well-known relationships Aphrodite has with mortals as described in ancient Greek myth and literature.

Pandora

The story of Pandora, the first mortal woman, is recounted by the poet Hesiod twice in his narrative poems, which were composed sometime in the eighth or seventh century BC. Hesiod describes the creation of Pandora in the *Works and Days* (54–105); he also tells the story of the first woman in a briefer version, and without naming her Pandora, in the *Theogony* (561–89). In the more well-known and detailed version told in the *Works and Days*, the first mortal woman is commissioned by the great god Zeus to punish mankind for the theft of divine fire, a crime committed on the humans' behalf by the rebellious Titan, Prometheus: the woman is a penalty because she bears with her a great storage jar, or *pithos*, filled with all the pains and troubles of the world (*Works and Days* 94–95). As Hesiod explains it, Zeus commands each of the gods to endow the newly made woman with an attribute to enhance either her cunning nature or her physical beauty, since he meant to make her irresistible to anyone who came into contact with her. After she is created, Hermes, the herald of the gods, gives her the name "Pandora," defined by the poet as "all gifts," since each of the Olympian deities gave her an attribute (*Works and Days* 80–82). Some scholars argue that Hesiod's explicatory etymology here may actually be an inversion, perhaps intended as ironic, of the name's original, more laudatory meaning, "all giver" (Lombardo 1993): the name "Pandora" would then suggest a more nurturing female figure who bestows gifts rather than receives them. This interpretation may be borne out by an alternate name for the first mortal woman, Anesidora, "She who Causes Gifts to Be Sent Up," that occurs on the tondo (interior) of an Attic white-ground *kylix* attributed to the Tarquinia painter (*ca.* 470–460 BC): the scene depicts the gods Athena and Hephaestus putting the finishing touches on a central female figure, above whose head is a label that reads "Anesidora." Thus, from the very outset, the primordial woman, Pandora, is an ambivalent symbol, one that conveys two conflicting, but not mutually exclusive, meanings: she is an alluring punishment, a destructive beauty, and ultimately a divine ruse that both gives and takes, or as Zeus smugly promises, "an evil men will love to embrace" (*Works and Days* 57–58). In the *Works and Days* version, Aphrodite plays an important role in preparing the brand new woman for her debut among humans, as the goddess is asked by Zeus to bestow her own unique contribution upon Pandora.

> Then he [Zeus] called Hephaistos
> And told him to hurry and knead some earth and water
> And put a human voice in it, and some strength,
> And to make the face like an immortal goddess' face
> And the figure like a beautiful, desirable virgin's.
> Then he told Athene to teach her embroidery and weaving,
> And Aphrodite golden to spill grace on her head
> And painful desire and knee-weakening anguish.
> And he ordered the quicksilver messenger, Hermes,
> To give her a bitchy mind and a cheating heart.
> That's what he told them, and they listened to Lord Zeus,
> Kronos' son. And right away famous old Gimpy
> Plastered up some clay to look like a shy virgin
> Just like Zeus wanted, and the Owl-Eyed Goddess
> Got her all dressed up, and the Graces divine
> And Lady Persuasion put some gold necklaces
> On her skin, and the Seasons (with their long, fine hair)
> Put on her head a crown of springtime flowers.
> Pallas Athena put on the finishing touches,
> And the quicksilver messenger put in her breast
> Lies and wheedling words and a cheating heart,
> Just like rumbling Zeus wanted. And the gods' own herald
> Put a voice in her, and he named that woman
> Pandora, because all the Olympians donated something,
> And she was a real pain for human beings.
>
> (*Works and Days* 60–82, trans. Lombardo, 1993)

In this passage, Zeus delegates several gods to do specific tasks in the preparation of the first mortal woman, and Aphrodite is explicitly charged with making Pandora both physically beautiful and sexually compelling. So Aphrodite is asked by Zeus to work within her primary fields of erotic expertise: adornment and attraction. First, Aphrodite is asked to "spill grace" *charin amphicheai* (*Works and Days* 65) down upon Pandora's head: note the allusion to liquidity implied by the Greek verb *cheō*, "to pour, shed, spill" (on the notion of alluring erotic liquidity: Cyrino 1995). The liquid image here suggests Aphrodite's ministrations may involve a beautifying oil or unguent applied to Pandora, and evokes the "ambrosial oil" Aphrodite uses to beautify herself elsewhere in the early Greek texts (*elaiōi ambrotōi*, hymn 5.61–62; *Odyssey*

8.364–65); the image also recalls the scene in the *Odyssey* where Athena cleanses and rejuvenates Penelope's face with Aphrodite's own "immortal beauty" (*kallei . . . ambrosiōi, Odyssey* 18.192–93). Aphrodite also "pours" two other attributes into the vessel that is the newly made Pandora, as the goddess confers upon her "painful desire and knee-weakening anguish" (*Works and Days* 66). In a Campanian red-figure neck *amphora* (*ca.* late fifth century BC), Pandora is illustrated as an actual *pithos* jar with a woman's head, underscoring her function as a container into which attributes are poured. These "gifts" from Aphrodite represent the punishing consequences of the first woman's divinely bestowed beauty: because of Aphrodite, Pandora's lovely appearance will invite mortals to experience a sexual longing that is physically debilitating and excruciating (on the ancient Greek notion of *eros* as harmful to the body: Carson 1986; Cyrino 1995). More than any of the other gods who help fashion the first woman, it is Aphrodite's principal mission to make Pandora into the ambivalent symbol Zeus intends her to be, "an evil men will love to embrace" (*Works and Days* 57–58), a new mortal figure both beautiful and dangerous.

While the key elements of Zeus' original directive to make Pandora "an embraceable evil" are naturally allocated to Aphrodite, goddess of love and beauty, it is the members of her immortal entourage who perform the actual adornment. After the first woman is molded from clay, the *Charites*, or Graces, join with *Peithō*, the personified Persuasion, to adorn Pandora with gold necklaces (*Works and Days* 73–74), while the *Horae*, the Hours or Seasons, encircle her head with a garland "of spring flowers" (*Works and Days* 74–75). In both Greek art and poetry, the goddess Persuasion is often depicted as an attendant or companion of Aphrodite (Rosenzweig 2004). Both the Graces and the Hours, as they do here with Pandora, groom and adorn Aphrodite in the earliest Greek texts. The Graces attend Aphrodite at her favorite shrine on the island of Cyprus, where they bathe the goddess, anoint her with oil and dress her in new clothing, both after she makes love to Ares (*Odyssey* 8.364–66), and before she seduces Anchises (hymn 5.61–65). Like the Graces, the Hours welcome Aphrodite on the beach at Cyprus, embellish her with dresses, jewelry and a golden crown, then escort her to join the gods (hymn 6.5–18); and together with the Graces, the Hours dye Aphrodite's clothing "in spring flowers" (*Cypria* fragment 6.1–2). Thus, by adorning Pandora, this team of beautifiers – the Graces, the Hours and Persuasion – not only function as extensions of Aphrodite as they carry out her assigned task, but they also give Pandora the "divine treatment," rendering her nearly a mortal version of Aphrodite: beautiful, powerful and sexually irresistible. The participation of the goddess and her elite entourage in preparing Pandora highlights Aphrodite's power as a goddess of beauty, just as it confirms her status as an important deity attended by specific named minor goddesses who serve as her agents of adornment. Aphrodite's direct involvement with the brand-new woman, Pandora, validates her divine capacity to create beauty and to arouse erotic longing in the mortal realm.

Paris and Helen

No pair of mortals was ever more loved by Aphrodite than Paris and Helen, whose erotic union was initiated by none other than Aphrodite herself. It was the goddess' intense love for them and her persistent involvement in their affairs that led to the Trojan War, the greatest military conflict ever depicted in Greek mythology, art and literature. Paris, also known as Alexandros, was the handsome younger prince of Troy when he fell madly in love with the superlatively beautiful Helen, the queen of Sparta, who was legally married to Menelaus. Under the overt instigation of Aphrodite, and later with her continuing collaboration and consent, the passionate but illicit love affair between Paris and Helen launched the Greek campaign against Troy. In terms of the *casus belli*, then, Aphrodite's action in bringing the lovers together is the immediate cause of the war; her affiliation with Paris and Helen thereby links Aphrodite to the realms of both love and warfare. Moreover, Aphrodite's intimate and long-term association with Paris and Helen establishes the geographical extent of her influence over the mortal world, stretching from Sparta in the southern Peloponnese all the way across the Aegean Sea to Troy in Asia Minor, while also clearly illustrating her relentless focus on the erotic *mixis* of the most notorious star-crossed lovers in the Western tradition.

The early part of this triangular story was once told in a work called the *Cypria* (now lost), which was one of the cycle of Greek epic poems composed after the *Iliad*, most likely in the seventh or sixth century BC. Its title refers to the prominent role of Aphrodite in the action of the narrative, which, as we know from later summaries, fragments and quotations, described several of the events leading up to the Trojan War. Many of the noteworthy episodes recounted in the *Cypria* center on Aphrodite's direct involvement in joining the lovers Paris and Helen together. In fact, the *Cypria* opens with Aphrodite's enthusiastic participation in the celebrated event known as the Judgment of Paris. This was a contest of beauty in which the three most splendid and high-status Olympian goddesses – Aphrodite, Hera and Athena – competed for the prize of a golden apple designated "for the most beautiful." Just from the mention of these three initial details, "beauty contest," "golden" and "apple," which encompass some of Aphrodite's most significant attributes and spheres of influence, the outcome of this legendary dispute should come as no surprise: Aphrodite is the triumphant winner. But because of his inevitable yet auspicious verdict, Paris became the favored mortal of Aphrodite, and he has to remind his brother, the Trojan crown prince, Hector, not to blame him for the goddess' constant partiality.

> "But don't throw golden Aphrodite's gifts in my face.
> We don't get to choose what the gods give us, you know,
> And we can't just toss their gifts aside."
>
> (*Iliad* 3.64–66, trans. Lombardo, 1997)

According to the *Cypria*, it all started at the wedding of the sea goddess Thetis to a mortal king named Peleus. This was the biggest and most lavish social event in Greek mythology, to which all the gods and goddesses were invited, except for one: Eris, the personification of discord. True to her name, Eris crashes the wedding party and angrily tosses among the guests a golden apple inscribed with the words "for the most beautiful": the word in Greek is the feminine superlative, "*kallistē.*" A major brawl erupted among the female deities in attendance at the festivities over who should be awarded the golden apple and thus be awarded the title "the most beautiful." Finally the argument came down to three claimants: Hera, Athena and Aphrodite. Zeus wisely decided not to have anything to do with this touchy competition between his wife and two of his daughters, so he sent his son Hermes down to earth with the contestants to find a suitable human judge to break the three-way tie. Hermes escorted the three goddesses to the wooded mountains above Troy, where he persuaded a surprised Paris to pronounce his famous judgment. Each goddess appeared before Paris and offered him a bribe in exchange for his favorable decision. A summary of an early part of the lost epic *Cypria* highlights these influential events that were the direct cause of the Trojan War.

> Strife [Eris] arrives while the gods are feasting at the marriage of Peleus and starts a dispute between Hera, Athena, and Aphrodite as to which of them is fairest. These three are led by Hermes at the command of Zeus to Alexandros [Paris] on Mount Ida for his decision, and Alexandros, lured by his promised marriage with Helen, decides in favor of Aphrodite.
>
> (*Cypria* fragment 1, trans. Evelyn-White, 1936)

The *Cypria* passage draws exclusive attention to Aphrodite's offer to Paris: when it was Aphrodite's turn, she promised to give him the love of the most beautiful woman in the world, Helen of Sparta. Aroused by this irresistible bait, the erotically inclined Paris awarded the golden apple to Aphrodite who thereafter favored the Trojan prince in all his endeavors; while Hera and Athena, according to Homer, displayed an unceasing hostility towards the Trojan race on account of Paris' insult (*Iliad* 24.25–30). It is at this point in the tale that Aphrodite either sends or accompanies Paris to claim his prize in Sparta, where he finds Helen inconveniently married to Menelaus. In Euripides' play, *Helen* (dated 412 BC), Helen says that Aphrodite took the beauty prize "at the price of my marriage" (*Helen* 1097). Even so, swayed by Aphrodite and enchanted by the foreign prince's glamour and sexual magnetism, Helen abandons her husband and child to run away with Paris to Troy, where the couple are welcomed into the royal family. The story not only demonstrates Aphrodite's formidable powers of erotic persuasion and her ability to merge lovers together, it also confirms the narrative basis for her close familiarity with the celebrity couple.

In Troy, Aphrodite keeps getting involved on the human level, both within the royal palace and on the battlefield; she also continues to exhibit her divine favoritism towards Paris and Helen, both as separate individuals and as an amorous pair. In book 3 of the *Iliad*, Homer opens another window onto the complexities of this three-way relationship, with its several overlapping vectors and crossings of mortal–immortal boundaries. Scholars note that in many respects this section of the *Iliad* seems to recall or reintroduce the events that took place back in Sparta when Aphrodite first compelled the erotic union of Paris and Helen, including some important episodes that were later recorded in the *Cypria*; thus, book 3 of the *Iliad* would function as a kind of textual flashback to that earlier mythological time frame (on the narrative "flashback" strategy: Friedrich 1978; Nagy 1996). One example of this flashback mode in book 3 would be the *monomachia* or "duel" between Menelaus and Paris, a scene which ostensibly evokes the original conflict between the two men with principal claims on Helen: her husband and her lover (3.324–82). In fact, it is Paris who proposes the man-to-man battle (3.67–75), revealing a rather brash overconfidence in his martial prowess due to his self-assured status as Aphrodite's favorite; so the assembled armies gladly declare a truce and swear solemn oaths that they will abide by the outcome of the winner-take-all contest (3.250–58). Yet Menelaus is unquestionably the better fighter, so during their combat Paris is knocked down and is about to be dragged away, when Aphrodite intervenes to save her handsome young darling from the Spartan's grasp.

> But Aphrodite, Zeus' daughter, had all this
> In sharp focus and snapped the oxhide chinstrap,
> Leaving Menelaus clenching an empty helmet . . .
>
> But Aphrodite
> Whisked Paris away with the sleight of a goddess
> Enveloping him in mist, and lofted him into
> The incensed air of his vaulted bedroom.

(Iliad 3.374–82, trans. Lombardo, 1997)

This episode highlights Aphrodite's deep and protective love for Paris, as she shields him from certain death at the hands of a superior warrior, Menelaus, while it also underscores an important aspect of her divinity: her close affiliation to warfare. The goddess carefully watches the duel "in sharp focus" (3.374); when her beloved Paris is threatened, Aphrodite does not shy away from the battlefield, but rushes into the mêlée to rescue him. Even more notably, her interference in the duel between Helen's husband and lover instantly ruptures the truce between the Greeks and the Trojans, so that Aphrodite's deed has the effect of initiating a new, bloodier and more intense phase of the war. But, in the relationship of Aphrodite to her favorite couple, Paris and Helen, war is inseparable from love. So at this point in the narrative of book 3, Aphrodite whisks Paris safely away, not back to his brother Hector and the other Trojan fighters on the combat line, but to his own "sweet-smelling bedroom" in the Trojan palace (3.382); the presence in the chamber of fragrance, a symbol of both divine and erotic elements, implies that Paris can expect a pleasant sexual encounter orchestrated by the goddess of love.

Next, Aphrodite turns her meddling attention to Helen, who is standing on the rampart surrounded by Trojan women and observing the battle (3.383–84). Just as she first brought Paris and Helen together in Sparta, Aphrodite will now unite them in Troy, as the "flashback" mechanism again unfolds in this sequence to integrate the narratives of past and present (Nagy 1996). To achieve her erotic objectives on the mortal plane, Aphrodite allows the war's grim present to become blurred with the romantic adventures of the past. Disguised as an old wool-working woman whom Helen loved dearly back in Sparta (3.385–89), and assuming the human role of matchmaker, Aphrodite coaxes Helen to go to meet her Trojan lover, drawing a tempting image of Paris' radiant good looks as he waits for her in their bed (3.390–94). For a moment, Helen sees Paris in her mind's eye as he must have appeared to her the first time, with Aphrodite as ardent instigator of their love affair. But Helen shakes off the nostalgic mirage, when she easily identifies the signature divine features of Aphrodite's body – her beautiful neck, lush breasts, and flashing eyes – shining out from under the masquerade (3.395–98). Though she is in deep awe of Aphrodite's supernatural appearance, Helen nevertheless recognizes the trick and chides the goddess with mocking familiarity, presuming the kind of intimacy shared between close friends or near equals.

> "You eerie thing, why do you love
> Lying to me like this? Where are you taking me now?
> Phrygia? Beautiful Maeonia? Another city
> Where you have some other boyfriend for me?
> Or is it because Menelaus, having just beaten Paris,
> Wants to take his hateful wife back to his house
> That you stand here now with treachery in your heart?
> Go sit by Paris yourself! Descend from the gods' high road,
> Allow your precious feet not to tread on Olympus,
> Go fret over him constantly, protect him.
> Maybe someday he'll make you his wife – or even his slave.
> I'm not going back there. It would be treason
> To share his bed. The Trojan women
> Would hold me at fault. I have enough pain as it is."
>
> (*Iliad* 3.399–412, trans. Lombardo, 1997)

Helen's audacious, even insolent, speech underscores the proximity, both physical and psychological, between herself and Aphrodite, since the Spartan queen readily transgresses the boundary between mortal and immortal by addressing the goddess in such a tart and familiar tone. Yet the speech illustrates several other noteworthy features of reciprocity in their relationship, as it reveals a provocative conflation of status between the two female figures. First, Helen acknowledges that she is being used as a divine instrument to further Aphrodite's erotic and military goals in the human realm (3.400–2), while the bitterness of her reproach is also an explicit self-condemnation of her own susceptibility to the temptation embodied by Aphrodite. Ironically, given her role as a notorious adulteress, Helen is also very concerned about appropriate conduct following her husband's victory over her lover in the duel, even as she realizes that Aphrodite opposes her return to Menelaus (3.403–5). Then, in an outrageous rebuke, Helen invites Aphrodite to relinquish her divinity and consummate her bond to Paris by suggesting the goddess assumes Helen's own ambiguous role as the Trojan's "wife – or even his slave" (3.409). Though Helen's derision here is obviously self-recriminating, she also exposes Aphrodite's intense attachment to and identification with the lovers, as well as her intimate relationships with mortals in general. Most remarkably, Helen blithely equates the goddess with herself. In her speech, Helen seems to imply both she and Aphrodite occupy a shared but elusive category of promiscuous or adulterous women, erotic "free agents" engaged in non-marital sexual activities who are not under the immediate supervision or control of men. Helen has indeed blurred a few lines.

It takes just a moment for an infuriated Aphrodite to make the boundaries clear again, as she reasserts her divinity with a stark threat.

> "Don't vex me, bitch, or I may let go of you
> And hate you as extravagantly as I love you now.
> I can make you repulsive to both sides, you know,
> Trojans and Greeks, and then where will you be?"

(Iliad 3.414–17, trans. Lombardo, 1997)

In her rejoinder, Aphrodite candidly articulates the bipolar nature of intense affect, with love and hate at either end of the emotional axis: "and [I will] hate you as extravagantly as I love you now" (3.415). As the goddess of the complementary spheres of love and war, Aphrodite also establishes her capacity to insert Helen in between the two warring sides, thereby making her vulnerable to the most dangerous sort of liminality (3.416–17). With a shudder, Helen obeys; and just as she left Sparta – quietly, unattended, and under the overwhelming compulsion of the goddess – she proceeds to join Paris in their bedroom (3.418–20). Although Aphrodite confirms her absolute superiority over the Spartan queen, it is interesting to note that Helen's direct paternity from the god Zeus is twice referred to in this passage ("Helen, born from Zeus" 3.418; "Helen, daughter of aegis-bearing Zeus" 3.426). Scholars observe that the congruence in epithets here may validate the notion that Helen was originally a local Spartan goddess, a variant or avatar of Aphrodite (Friedrich 1978). Or perhaps the poet simply wished to remind his audience that Helen, like Aphrodite, is also a child of Zeus, and, as the passage makes evident, both Helen and Aphrodite are beautiful, irresistible and volatile figures. At the end of book 3 of the Iliad, the goddess succeeds in fusing Helen and Paris together again, as their lovemaking merges past and present times to achieve Aphrodite's divine purpose of erotic and martial mixis (3.421–46). These early Greek texts reveal that the lovers, Helen and Paris, enjoyed an unquestionable privilege as two of Aphrodite's most favored mortals in Greek mythology, and her intimate affiliation with them lays bare her divine dominion over the realms of love and warfare.

Anchises and Aeneas

Aphrodite's familiarity with mortals and her involvement on the human plane sometimes takes on a more personal erotic aspect. The story of Aphrodite's sexual union with the mortal Anchises, a member of the Dardanian branch of the Trojan royal house, is told in the *Homeric Hymn to Aphrodite* (hymn 5), which was probably composed sometime in the late seventh century BC (most recently, with meticulous commentary and thorough review of scholarship: Faulkner 2008). In Greek myth and literature, Trojan males had a reputation for being exceptionally good-looking and sexually alluring, so much so that their beauty and charisma often got them involved in high-level erotic adventures. As we have seen, the handsome Paris, prince of Troy, fulfilled his destined love for Helen, with Aphrodite's help, which led to the great Trojan War; the royal Trojan boy, Ganymede, son of the early king Tros, was so beautiful, he was abducted by Zeus and taken to live on Olympus to serve as his divine cup-bearer; and Tithonus, brother of the Trojan king Priam, and thus Paris' uncle, was loved by Eos, goddess of the dawn. In the hymn, Aphrodite herself admiringly cites this trait among the men of Troy to explain her powerful sexual attraction to Anchises.

> "Your family, though, among all mortal people,
> Are closest to the gods in their appearance."
>
> (hymn 5.200–1, trans. Ruden, 2005)

The fifth Homeric hymn offers a stirring narrative of the goddess' erotic rendezvous with Anchises, who worked as a rugged cattleman on the lush slopes of Mt. Ida in Troy. The cause of their love affair is stated near the beginning of the hymn. As retribution for her unremitting activity of blending gods with mortals in sexual *mixis*, as well as for constantly boasting about it (45–52), Zeus causes the goddess to feel a fierce desire for the handsome mortal Trojan.

> And so he made her hanker for Anchises.
> Among the many springs of Ida's tall peaks
> He herded cows in all his godlike beauty.
> When humorous Aphrodite got her first look,
> She fell in love – her mind was gone completely.
>
> (hymn 5.53–57, trans. Ruden, 2005)

Critics have long argued about the purpose and significance of Zeus' erotic intervention early on in the narrative of the hymn: some scholars maintain that Zeus intends to humiliate Aphrodite by joining her sexually with a mortal in an attempt to undermine her pervasive influence, while others see a rather ironic inversion of authority in the tale that ultimately serves to confirm Aphrodite's awesome power (on the shame/power inversion motif: Cyrino 1993). Many scholars observe how the passage focuses chiefly on Aphrodite's relentless practice of blurring the physical boundaries between gods and humans: far from suggesting any trace of sexual embarrassment or jealousy, the hymn instead shows the goddess' expertise in negotiating the two poles of the mortal–immortal axis (Smith 1981; Clay 1989). If Zeus indeed meant to shame the goddess by forcing her into sexual activity with a gorgeous human hero, one who "resembled the immortal gods in his body" (55), it appears Aphrodite had no problem whatsoever playing along with her punishment. The goddess of love immediately prepares herself to seduce Anchises, so first she goes to her sanctuary at Paphos on the island of Cyprus for her *kosmēsis*, to bathe and dress (58–67). Next, Aphrodite reaches the peak of Mt. Ida in Troy, where she effortlessly inhabits a liminal space halfway between the immortal and mortal worlds (68–69). This mountain top is an appropriate location for Aphrodite's mission of erotic mingling: it was here that Hera seduced Zeus during the Trojan War (*Iliad* 14.153–360). To facilitate her passage into this interstitial territory where Anchises dwells, and just as she did when she approached Helen on the ramparts in Troy (*Iliad* 3.386–89), the goddess decides to assume a disguise.

Aphrodite's artful epiphany before Anchises highlights the remarkable double exposure of their meeting. When the goddess arrives at the secluded huts of the herdsmen (75–80), she finds Anchises – unsuspecting and all alone (76, 79) – and looking extraordinarily handsome: the hymn describes him as "a hero with beauty from the gods" (77). Scholars note Anchises is here presented as an ambiguous figure, since he is a "godlike" mortal and a cattleman working on the borders between civilization and the outback, so his status is somewhere between supernatural and human (Clay 1989). As a match for this ambiguity, Aphrodite takes on the appearance of a tall, beautiful mortal virgin, both to assuage his fears and to arouse his sexual desire (81–83). But the goddess' disguise poses a crisis of perception for Anchises (Bergren 1989): is she really human or is she a goddess? It is at this point, as we have discussed earlier, that the hymn offers the most elaborate and detailed description of Aphrodite's costume, with all her accessories and ornaments, at the moment when Anchises first lays his eyes upon her (84–90). Amid her bright clothing and gleaming jewelry, a celestial glow emanated from Aphrodite's signature physical feature, her lovely breasts, whose radiance is elsewhere in Greek literature unmistakable even under a disguise (to Helen: *Iliad* 3.396–97), and the very place where she keeps the erotic charm, the magic *himas*, an embroidered leather thong that inspires sexual lust (*Iliad* 14.214–15). No wonder, then, that her shimmering beauty leads Anchises, overwhelmed by desire, to presume the maiden's identity is divine (91–99); he even includes the correct guess: "Are you golden Aphrodite?" (93). After promising to build her a sacred altar on the mountain top, the hero requests her divine blessing for himself and his family (100–6). Anchises may be only a mortal, but he thinks he knows a goddess when he sees one.

Yet fun-loving Aphrodite has no intention of letting the ruse slip, so she delivers a sexy speech veiled in a veneer of innocence, but full of ambiguous language and teasing allusions (107–42). First, the "daughter of Zeus" (107) – note the hymn's ironic use of the epithet to describe the disguised deity (Boedeker 1974) – brazenly denies she is a goddess at all, but rather insists she is a mortal girl born of noble Phrygian parents (109–12). Like the expert seductress she is, Aphrodite fills her deceptive speech with enough factual detail and flattery to persuade her listener. She even explains why she speaks Anchises' language, spinning an elaborate tale about having a Trojan nurse as a child (113–16): note that this is one of the earliest texts to observe differences in *glōssa* or "language" (Smith 1981; Rayor 2004; see also the reference to the different languages of the Trojan allies at *Iliad* 2.803–6). With girlish excitement, she tells Anchises she was just snatched up by the god Hermes from a ritual celebration of Artemis (117–21): note how the verbal image of lithe maidens dancing in a community ritual, as well as the cunning use of the erotic abduction motif, underscore Aphrodite's intent to attract Anchises by her presentation of youth, beauty and sexual availability (on the titillating aspects of her speech: Bergren 1989; Clay 1989; Rayor 2004; Faulkner 2008). As she rounds off her remarks with a proposal for marriage, Aphrodite skilfully seals the seduction by again emphasizing her erotic inexperience, implying she is just waiting to be initiated by Anchises: "Before you've done it, while I'm still a virgin [literally: 'untamed,' *admētēn*], take me to meet your father and your mother" (133–34, trans. Ruden, 2005). Just like that, Aphrodite's persuasive, coquettish speech hits its target.

While Anchises' response clearly reveals his caution, he is overcome with intense and immediate sexual longing, struck hard by Aphrodite's carefully aimed shot of *glukus himeros*, "sweet desire" (143). Anchises even implicitly acknowledges his defeat in the contest when he vows to have sex with her – shrewdly addressing her as "lady who looks like the goddesses" (153) – even if he is shot dead by Apollo the archer and sent down to Hades (149–54). But this is a false resolution, for Anchises doesn't die. Instead, the hymn allows him an expression of his physical power and skills, as he takes the goddess by the hand and leads her, with her beautiful eyes cast demurely down, to his bed.

> He took her hand. The laughter-loving goddess
> First shied away and looked down with her sweet eyes,
> Then stole into the well-made bed. Soft blankets
> Lay on it for the hero, and above them
> Were skins of bears and deep-voiced lions slaughtered
> By the young man himself on the towering mountains.
> The two got on the well-constructed bedstead.
>
> (hymn 5.155–61, trans. Ruden, 2005)

Although the eye-lowering gesture has been variously interpreted by critics (e.g. shame: van Eck 1978; feigned hesitation. Smith 1981; sign of unreal wedding ceremony: Bergren 1989; attempt to conceal divinity: Clay 1989), it seems most likely the goddess lets her gaze fall so her lover doesn't see the self-satisfied gleam of victory in her eyes (Faulkner 2008). Covering Anchises' bed are the skins of ferocious bears and lions he has slain in the forest (158–60), offering visible symbols of the man's courage, prowess and control over nature (Rayor 2004). This descriptive detail of the animal skins provides an image that balances the status differential between the boundary-blurring lovers, Aphrodite and Anchises, as it creates a temporarily level space before the act of erotic blending between the goddess of such potency and the mortal she has just overpowered. Now the Trojan strips off every item of Aphrodite's shining raiment, all her jewelry and clothing, echoing in reverse order the earlier description of her *kosmēsis* when she first appeared before Anchises (84–90). Perhaps the removal of her attire also suggests a leveling of the status hierarchy between them, or it may simply indicate the required revelation of Aphrodite's essential naked beauty before lovemaking. But there is one added detail, as Anchises also undoes her *zōnē*, or "belt" (164): the removal of Aphrodite's *zōnē* here is a clear signal of her surrender to sexual activity with Anchises. In this seduction, both lovers achieve their amorous goals, proving both humans and gods are engaged in the compelling *mixis* inspired by Aphrodite. Moreover, the strongly marked eroticism of this narrative articulates the hymn's fundamental purpose: to explore the erotic intersections between mortal and immortal that the goddess of love instigates and over which she holds sway.

After lovemaking, Aphrodite resumes her divine aspect and presents herself in full goddess mode to Anchises (168–80). Though terrified at first, Anchises is reassured by Aphrodite in a long speech (191–290), in which she promises that the sexual blending they just enjoyed will be fruitful: beneath her *zōnē*, she tells him, she is carrying his child (255). Their son will be named Aeneas (198), and as the explicit emblem of their cross-status erotic coupling, the boy will be "very much like a god" (279). Like his father, Anchises, the godlike cattleman, and his mother, the goddess who actively intervenes in the mortal realm, the hero Aeneas will partake of both divine and human attributes. After five years, Aeneas, conceived by a goddess and raised by the nymphs of the wilderness, will go to Troy to join his mortal father and the other noble men of Troy (273–80). Thus, the birth of Aeneas symbolizes the potential for human communion with the divine, a sacred *mixis* or mingling achieved in this hymn through a story of seduction where immortal and mortal, victor and vanquished, are not always readily discernible one from the other. The story of Aphrodite's love for Anchises codifies the very blurring of erotic boundaries that is consecrated to the goddess.

Aphrodite's maternal affiliation to Aeneas is mentioned elsewhere in the early Greek texts, as Hesiod describes the goddess' tryst with the Trojan, Anchises, and their resulting offspring.

> And Kythereia, beautifully crowned, bore Aineias,
> After mingling in sweet love with the hero Anchises
> On the peaks above Ida's many wooded glens.
>
> (*Theogony* 1008–10, trans Lombardo, 1993)

Aeneas is also named as the son of Aphrodite and Anchises in book 2 of the *Iliad*, where the poet records a catalog of warriors who fought in the great Trojan War.

> The Dardanian troops were led by Aeneas,
> Whom bright Aphrodite bore to Anchises,
> A goddess lying with a mortal man
> In the foothills of Ida.
>
> (*Iliad* 2.819–21, trans. Lombardo, 1997)

But Aphrodite's main appearance with her son Aeneas in the early Greek texts occurs during the Trojan warrior's participation in the extended and bloody fighting sequence of book 5 of the *Iliad* (5.166–453). Just as she did when she rescued Paris from certain doom in his duel with Menelaus (*Iliad* 3.324–82), the goddess again hurries down to the plain to save a vulnerable favorite. Here, her beloved son Aeneas is under violent attack by a pack of marauding Greeks, and is seriously injured: his hip socket is smashed by a slab of stone wielded by the Greek hero

Diomedes (5.297–310). As the stricken Trojan sinks to the ground, his mother rushes in to help him.

That would have been the end of Aeneas,
But his mother, Aphrodite, Zeus' daughter,
Who bore Aeneas to Anchises the oxherd,
Had all this in sharp focus. Her milk-white arms
Circled around him and she enfolded him
In her radiant robe to prevent the Greeks
From killing him with a spear to the chest.

(*Iliad* 5.312–17, trans. Lombardo, 1997)

In this safeguarding scene, Aphrodite wraps her son Aeneas in the folds of her shining *peplos*, or "dress" (5.315), while during her earlier rescue of Paris, the goddess enveloped him "in a thick mist" (*ēeri pollēi*, 3.381). The detail is noteworthy, because the poet mentions the dress again as the target of an assault against the goddess. As she is carrying her son from the battlefield, Aphrodite is wounded by Diomedes, who thrusts his spear into her wrist, just above the palm, stabbing her through the folds of her dress sleeve (5.330–42): this is the same "immortal dress" made for her by her attendants, the Graces (5.338). With her hand hurt and her gown ripped, Aphrodite abruptly lets Aeneas drop (5.342); so the god, Apollo, who also favors the Trojan side, lunges in and saves the injured warrior, gathering him up "in a dark blue cloud" (*kuaneēi nephelēi*, 5.344–45). What we learn from this scene is that evidently the supernatural cloud or mist is a more effective salvation mechanism than a dress, even a divine bespoke one, which provides rather feeble protection for the goddess and none for her son, whom she is trying to shield from harm. So while Aphrodite does not hesitate to enter the field of combat to save Aeneas, her military defense endeavor here falls short.

But this failed rescue scene on the epic battlefield also raises the question of Aphrodite's maternal relationship to her child: is she a "good mother" or not? Though it appears Aphrodite makes every effort to exhibit maternal care for her son, Aeneas, her lack of capacity for follow-through in this passage is significant, especially since she was able to protect Paris successfully in the comparable rescue scene in *Iliad* book 3. Later in the story of the war, Aphrodite displays loving care for Hector's corpse, keeping the dogs at bay by anointing the body with immortal oil of rose (*Iliad* 23.185–87). In the incident with Aeneas, however, not only does Aphrodite fail to protect her son, but Apollo is obliged to come in and finish the task. It should also be noted in the narrative of the fifth Homeric hymn (discussed above) that Aphrodite essentially declares she will abandon her half-mortal son during the formative years of his infancy and childhood to the care of the mountain nymphs (hymn 5.256–75). Episodes such as these have led some scholars to argue that Aphrodite is not a kourotrophic deity at all, that is, she is not a nurturer of boys in particular or children in general: this task in Greek mythology usually falls to the elite virgin goddesses, such as Athena or Artemis, or occasionally to Apollo (Budin 2003). Thus, it is not surprising to find Aphrodite's maternity downplayed in her myths, and in fact, she is often strongly marked in the earliest Greek texts by a deficiency of maternal concern towards her offspring. While Aphrodite's relationship to Aeneas implies her eager involvement in the martial milieu of the Trojan battle-field, it also demonstrates the collapse of her maternal attention towards him and her inability to follow through in her care for her son.

Adonis

The mortal youth, Adonis, was famous in Greek mythology for his stun-ning and almost other-worldly physical beauty. Indeed, the name "Adonis" remains a byword even today to describe an extremely hand-some man. One of the most significant and influential narratives about Aphrodite's liaisons with mortals to emerge in later Greek literature is the tale of her love affair with Adonis and her grief over his untimely death. Since the love story appears rather late in the Greek sources, there exist several variants with many contradictory details recorded by differ-ent authors, but a basic outline can be discerned. Adonis was a beautiful noble boy, whose parentage is variously given. In some accounts, Adonis is the son of Cinyras of Cyprus, while in others his father is named as Thias, king of Assyria; while his mother's name is usually given as Smyrna, or Myrrha (summary in Apollodorus, *The Library* 3.14.3–4). The generally accepted version of his miraculous birth is as follows. Aphrodite became angry over Smyrna's refusal to worship her; and so as punishment, the goddess subjected the girl to an incestuous sexual pas-sion for her own father. Through a ruse, Smyrna slept with her unwitting father for several nights in a row and became pregnant. When her father discovered what had happened, he was outraged and pursued Smyrna with a sword, intending to kill her. As she ran away and hid in the forest, the gods – by some reports, Aphrodite herself – heard her pleas and turned her into a myrrh tree, or in later accounts, a myrtle tree. After ten months, the tree burst open, and Adonis was born.

Because of his exquisite beauty, Aphrodite took the baby and con-cealed him in a chest, entrusting her secret only to the goddess

Persephone, queen of the Underworld, whom she asked for help in protecting the child. But when Persephone saw him, she also became enamored of his loveliness and refused to give him back to Aphrodite. In some versions of the tale, the custody dispute between the two goddesses is resolved by Zeus, while in other accounts, Calliope, the head muse, provided the arbitration. The case was settled by dividing the year into three parts: Adonis was to spend one third of the year with each goddess and the last third he could spend with whomever he chose. Naturally, this meant that he spent two-thirds of the year with Aphrodite, who soon took him as her lover. This state of affairs lasted until the youth's sudden death.

One day while Adonis was hunting, he was gored by the tusk of a wild boar. This was no accident: the boar was either sent by Ares, the god of war who is Aphrodite's jealous lover, or alternatively by the goddess Artemis, angry over the punishment of her own favorite mortal, Hippolytus. Aphrodite rushed to the side of the fatally wounded youth and Adonis died in her arms. From the drops of his blood mingled with her tears came the short-lived *anemone*, or "wind flower"; some say the goddess wounded herself on a thorn and her own blood colored the red rose. Thus, the myth of Adonis offers etiologies for Aphrodite's floral symbols; as the travel writer Pausanias notes: "The rose and the myrtle are sacred to Aphrodite and connected with the story of Adonis" (*Description of Greece* 6.24.7). After his death, Adonis forever joined Persephone in the Underworld, and Aphrodite mourned long and deeply the loss of her beautiful beloved. The Greek poet Bion (*ca.* 100 BC), who hailed from Smyrna in Asia Minor but spent most of his life in Sicily, recounted Aphrodite's anguish over the death of Adonis in a lyric mythological poem.

> Adonis has a savage, savage wound on his thigh,
> but Cytherea carries a greater wound in her heart.
> Around that boy his dear hounds bay
> and mountain nymphs weep. But Aphrodite,
> having let down her hair, rushes through the woods
> mourning, unbraided, unsandalled; and the thorns
> cut her as she goes and pluck sacred blood.
> Shrilly wailing, through long winding dells she wanders,
> crying out the Assyrian cry, calling her consort and boy.
> Around her floated the dark robe at her navel;
> her chest was made scarlet by her hands; the breasts below
> snowy before, grew crimson for Adonis.
> "Alas for Cytherea!" mourn the Loves in reply.

(*Lament for Adonis* 16–28, trans. Reed, 1997)

Before assuming the role of Aphrodite's doomed mortal paramour in Greek mythology, Adonis may have been playing a key part in the mystery cults of antiquity. Adonis is a complex and enigmatic hero/god figure of West Semitic origin, whose name is a variation of the Semitic title *adon*, meaning "lord." Even with its many mythological variants, the story of Adonis seems to represent an example of the ancient Mediterranean narrative pattern of the hero/god who alternates his time in the upper and lower worlds. Earlier scholarship tended to interpret this to mean that Adonis was closely related to deities of death and rebirth, widespread in ancient cultures across North Africa and the Near East, whose myths serve as analogies for the seasonal cycle of vegetation. However, it is more accurate to compare the Adonis story to the ritual mourning associated with the tales of the Sumerian hero/god Dumuzi (Tammuz) whose death is lamented by his lover, the goddess Inanna. The traditional narrative connection of Adonis with Assyria may well be due to the notion that the cult of Adonis had originated in Assyria, or perhaps in Babylonia, where he was worshipped as Tammuz, and was later introduced into Greek mythology as Adonis; the link to the island of Cyprus may indicate the direction from which the cult of Adonis arrived in Greece, as well as reinforcing the mythological relationship of Adonis to his divine consort, Aphrodite, the Cyprian goddess. In the myth of Adonis, the annual alternating custody deal between Aphrodite and Persephone, queen of the dead, reveals that Adonis is a figure who splits his time between the upper and lower worlds, and who is ritually mourned at the moment of his mortal transition.

In classical Greek times, the cult of Adonis was celebrated mainly by women in the Adonia, the midsummer festival that commemorated Aphrodite's grief over the death of her lover, Adonis (most recently, on Aphrodite and the Adonia: Rosenzweig 2004). The festival seems to have become popular in Athens by the mid-fifth century BC, though the cult of Adonis appears to be mentioned by the poet Sappho (fragment 140a), so similar rites may also have been observed in Lesbos as early as the sixth century BC. During the heat of the dog days of July, the Adonia were celebrated in private homes by women of all social classes, including courtesans, who often invited their lovers. At the start of the festival, the celebrating women would plant "gardens of Adonis" (*kēpoi Adōnidos*) in small baskets or shallow broken pots. These "gardens" were composed of quick-growing plants, like fennel and lettuce, as well as grains of wheat and barley that rapidly sprang from seed. The women would take the little gardens up onto the rooftops of their houses – which they reached by climbing ladders – where the sun burned hottest against the stucco. And just like the beautiful youth Adonis, the plants would sprout in the heat and then wither and die quickly, while the women, in imitation of Aphrodite, would mourn openly and noisily for the premature death of the goddess' lover (Detienne 1972). The ladder, or *klimax* in Greek, functioned as an important emblem in the rites of the Adonia, and several Athenian vase paintings from this period depict scenes of women perched upon ladders while holding shallow pots: the ladder not only allowed the women to pass from their daily lives of domestic routine up into the open-air realm of euphoric religious experience, it also symbolized Adonis' own sudden transition from one state of existence to another (on the artistic iconography of the ladder: Rosenzweig 2004). Since the ladder bridges the gap between the two separate worlds, mortal and immortal, it serves as the physical symbol of the *mixis* or erotic fusion instigated by Aphrodite in her boundary-crossing desire for the human boy. In the next stage of the Adonia, the women would celebrate with feasting, wine and merriment, in joyous tribute to Adonis' annual return from the land of the dead, and his loving welcome back into Aphrodite's tender embrace.

PUNISHMENT

Just as Aphrodite became angry over Smyrna's refusal to worship her and so punished the girl by filling her with an incestuous sexual passion for her own father, there were other mortals who foolishly scorned the goddess of love and thus suffered her wrath and retribution. In the Greek mythological and literary tradition, the punishment myth motif serves as a narrative warning to humans of their solemn obligation to honor the gods, while it also functions as a strong deterrent against any arrogant or imprudent behavior that might offend them. As the goddess of sexuality, Aphrodite represents the intense emotional drive towards erotic *mixis* and the blurring of physical margins in the sexual act. Though the ancient Greeks considered the erotic experience undeniably pleasurable, it was also regarded as an inherently dangerous sensation that posed the threat of bodily dissolution and mental infirmity to those who indulged in love (Cyrino 1995). Hesiod describes the powerful effect of Eros *lusimelēs*, "the limb-loosener," a god who "makes their bodies . . . go limp, mastering their minds and subduing their wills" (*Theogony* 120–22, trans. Lombardo, 1993). It is no surprise, then, that some mortals are afraid of damaging or even losing their personal boundaries, a fear that causes them to reject unwisely Aphrodite's erotic blessing. Thus, there are several cautionary tales in Greek myth and literature of mortals simply refusing to engage these passions, or of their insolent and

INTIMACY WITH MORTALS   99

ultimately doomed attempts to suppress the influence of Aphrodite altogether. While Aphrodite mingles freely and willingly with mortals, showering those who worship her with love, beauty and success, those who would deny her divinity are punished with hate, ugliness, and sometimes even death. Aphrodite often exquisitely crafts her penalties to "fit the crime" committed by these reckless, impious mortals.

One famous example of Aphrodite's incisive wrath is the tale of the women of Lemnos, an island in the Aegean Sea (as told by Apollonius of Rhodes, *Argonautica* 1.609–39; also a summary in Apollodorus, *The Library* 1.9.17). The Lemnian women dishonored Aphrodite by denying her due offerings, so the goddess afflicted them with a foul stench so disgusting that their husbands refused to have sex with them. Note the terrible irony here: the goddess of lovely fragrance, who uses perfume to allure lovers, curses these disrespectful women with a revolting smell that repels their sexual partners. When their husbands turned to their Thracian captives for erotic satisfaction, the Lemnian women became enraged with jealousy, and so they murdered the entire male population (along with the slave girls). Soon afterwards, with the approval of Aphrodite, the island is fortunately repopulated when the Greek hero Jason and his crew of Argonauts spend their sailors' shore leave with the by now sex-starved women: as the poet Apollonius of Rhodes tells us, Jason himself sleeps with Hypsipyle, the queen of Lemnos (*Argonautica* 1.842–64). This time, the women are mindful enough to celebrate Aphrodite with thank-offerings in gratitude for her erotic bounty.

Hippolytus

The most infamous tale of Aphrodite's vengeful ire towards a mortal is the story of the abstemious youth, Hippolytus, told in Euripides' tragedy *Hippolytus*, which was produced on the Athenian stage at the City Dionysia in 428 BC (on the play: Barrett 1964; Goff 1990; Mills 2002). The narrative of this masterful drama offers an austere portrayal of the extraordinary risks involved in human interactions with the divine, while also highlighting the treacherous rivalries such boundary-crossing relationships can provoke among the immortals themselves. In Euripides' play, Aphrodite is determined to punish the young virgin Hippolytus, who abstains from any sexual contact – the ancient Greeks would have deemed this celibate behavior quite peculiar for an elite young man (Zeitlin 1996) – and thus blatantly denies her divine power, while at the same time he worships only the virgin goddess Artemis. Thus, the drama underscores an oppositional model of female divinity where the goddesses occupy two very separate, distinct, and even incompatible realms of experience. Certainly, the goddesses couldn't be more different: the virginity of the huntress, Artemis, can be seen as a physical articulation of her remoteness and aloof nature as depicted in her myths, while her lack of expressed sexuality stands in direct contrast to the intimacy, familiarity and promiscuity represented by the uniquely extroverted Aphrodite.

Since there can be no happy middle ground between abstinence and indulgence, it is evident from the outset of the drama that Hippolytus has chosen the virgin's side. An infuriated Aphrodite, though she appears only in the prologue of the play, makes it very clear that she will not be snubbed by a mere mortal, as she complains bitterly about the insult dealt to her by the obstinate, foolish youth Hippolytus. Between Aphrodite and Artemis, total acquiescence and total denial, the concept of *timē*, "honor," is strictly a zero-sum game: if you worship just one goddess, the other by definition suffers a corresponding loss of tribute. Aphrodite elucidates all this in the opening words of the prologue.

> "Powerful, well-known throughout the earth
> and in the heavens, I am the goddess called
> Cypris. All who live and see the light
> from Pontus to the Pillars of the west
> revere my power and receive their due –
> or, if they scorn me, I can make them pay.
> For gods, like men, crave honor and respect;
> they revel in the worship they receive.
>
> "Soon enough I'll prove that this is true.
> Theseus' child, the son of the Amazon,
> the protégé of godly Pittheus,
> Hippolytus, alone of the citizens
> of Troezen, of this land, claims that I am
> the very worst of all divinities.
> He renounces sex, recoils from marriage, honors
> only Phoebus' sister, Zeus' daughter
> Artemis, whom he believes to be
> the very greatest of divinities.
> He is with the virgin goddess constantly;
> racing through the woodlands with his dogs,
> he depletes the wild forest of its game
> while he enjoys a camaraderie
> greater than what mortals might expect.

I don't begrudge the two of them. What for?
Where I'm concerned, however, Hippolytus
will find he has miscalculated badly;
and I will make him pay for it, before
this day is out."

(*Hippolytus* 1–22, trans. Svarlien, 2007)

What is unmistakable in Aphrodite's speech is the stark economic con-
tour of the divine–mortal relationship: if Hippolytus venerates Artemis
exclusively, Aphrodite is devalued, and this is simply intolerable. The
youth's deliberate dismissal of the cult of the goddess of love, and his
rejection of the entire sexual realm over which Aphrodite holds sway, are
classic symptoms of the self-deluded *hubris*, or "arrogant presumption,"
that in Greek mythology and literature always draws swift and sure com-
pensatory punishment. In the remainder of the prologue, Aphrodite
calmly explains her strategy of revenge. The goddess has already caused
the youth's stepmother, Phaedra, to fall madly in love with him: as Aphrodite describes it, when Phaedra first saw Hippolytus, she "felt Desire's
dreadful choking grip around her heart, according to my plan" (27–28,
trans. Svarlien, 2007). Phaedra's quasi-incestuous passion for her stepson – note the analogy with the story of Smyrna's unnatural lust – initi-
ates a disastrous trajectory that will lead to the death of Hippolytus at the
hands of his father, the Athenian hero Theseus: "And this young man,
my enemy, will be killed by his father" (43–44, trans. Svarlien, 2007). Just
as the goddess promises, the audience will be witnesses as Phaedra
becomes the unwitting vehicle of Aphrodite's terrible wrath. At first
ashamed of her illicit erotic desire for Hippolytus, and then incensed
and humiliated over his rebuff of her overtures (through a third party,
her nurse), Phaedra accuses the youth to Theseus of attempting to rape
her (on the familiar folk-tale motif of "Potiphar's wife": Barrett 1964). But
Phaedra makes the awful allegation upon a grim tableau of evidence: she
attaches a note incriminating Hippolytus to her body, and then hangs
herself. The fact that Phaedra commits suicide during Aphrodite's punishment of the defiant youth is considered merely collateral damage to
the goddess' ruthless purpose.

"Phaedra may keep her virtuous reputation
undiminished; still, she is destroyed.
Her suffering will not deter me from
the vengeance I will take on those I hate.
I'll do what I must do to make it right."

(*Hippolytus* 47–50, trans. Svarlien, 2007)

As the play unfolds its inexorable action, the severe penalty for rejecting an intimate alliance with Aphrodite becomes manifest. Theseus, believing Phaedra's brutal accusation, curses Hippolytus with one of the wishes granted to him by his own immortal father, Poseidon, the great god of the sea (885–90). As Hippolytus leaves the city in exile, Poseidon sends an immense bull from the sea to assail him: the monstrous sea bull, a symbol of the full-grown male sexuality that Hippolytus disavows, panics the youth's horses, and they bolt, dashing the chariot against the cliffs and dragging him all along the rocky shoreline (1173–254). Artemis also arrives on the scene and reveals the truth of the preceding events to Theseus (1283–341), just as Hippolytus' broken body is brought back to his father (1342–90). Though Artemis is bizarrely unmoved by the imminent death of her devoted mortal servant (1396), she is openly perturbed by the fact that Aphrodite trumped her in this round of their rivalry: "Cypris plotted this outrageous crime!" (1400, trans. Svarlien, 2007). So the virgin goddess promises to get back at Aphrodite for punishing her favorite, Hippolytus, and thereby perpetuates the divine cycle of retribution.

> "Don't worry: Cypris' plans,
> her anger, which has splintered your poor body,
> will not go unpunished, though you dwell
> in the gloom beneath the earth. I shall reward
> your piety, your uncorrupted mind.
> And I'll exact a price from Aphrodite:
> these arrows, which are inescapable,
> will strike whatever mortal she loves most."
>
> (*Hippolytus* 1416–22, trans. Svarlien, 2007)

With her words, Artemis acknowledges Aphrodite's frequent and familiar relationships with humans, as she vows to attack the one among them whom "she loves most" (1421). Most scholars agree the human victim Artemis is referring to in this speech can be none other than Adonis, the beautiful mortal lover of Aphrodite, who is fatally wounded during a boar hunt (e.g. Barrett 1964; Mills 2002; Svarlien 2007); in this they are following the ancient version of the tale that says it was Artemis who sent the boar to kill Adonis to avenge the death of Hippolytus (as in Apollodorus, *The Library* 3.14.4). While the conflict between the goddesses continues unresolved, the mortals whom they love are fatally touched by their close bonds with the divine. Aphrodite's harsh reprisal against Hippolytus and his renunciation of sex demonstrates her relentless defense of erotic *mixis* in the face of anyone who would challenge its universal power. Without a doubt, Aphrodite takes this one personally.

OVERVIEW

Each of Aphrodite's interactions with mortals corresponds in some significant way to a particular aspect of Aphrodite's divinity. In contributing to the creation of Pandora, the first mortal woman, Aphrodite expresses her expertise in the process of adornment and beautification, as well as her capacity to imbue Pandora with the power of erotic allure. Aphrodite's doting attachment to the celebrity couple, Paris and Helen, whose adulterous love affair caused the great Trojan War, epitomizes her divine mandate over the utterly entangled realms of love and warfare. The story of Aphrodite's sexual union with the cattleman Anchises exposes her own vulnerability to the border-crossing force of erotic desire, while her inability to care for their half-human son Aeneas reveals Aphrodite's essentially non-maternal character. In her famous love affair with the gorgeous youth Adonis, celebrated in the rebirth rites of the Adonia, Aphrodite confirms her divine power to blur boundaries across the mortal–immortal axis. Finally, Aphrodite's punishment of Hippolytus, the virgin boy who rejected her, proves the sheer folly of trying to deny the impulse towards the erotic *mixis* that Aphrodite inspires in every living thing.

6

SEA AND SKY

In this chapter, we will reflect on Aphrodite's unique nature as a goddess who shares in and rules over two vast elemental realms, the sea and the sky. As the goddess of *mixis*, or "mingling," Aphrodite's close affinity with the two disparate but contiguous spheres represents her role as a mediator, whose divine influence allows sea and sky to interact and converge with each other. We will examine the different aspects and meanings of Aphrodite's marine and celestial attributes, and observe how her benevolent presence has the effect of calming the stormy realms of sea and sky in ways that are advantageous to her human favorites. Furthermore, we will consider how Aphrodite's dominion over sea and sky expresses her universal, all-encompassing power, implying that the entire natural world lies under the goddess' control. This chapter will demonstrate how the marine and celestial image clusters ascribed to the goddess clearly reveal Aphrodite's embrace of polyvalence in her divine function and purpose.

ANODOS

Aphrodite exists in the interval where sea and sky meet, touch and mingle together. This in-between open space is at once delineated and joined together by the process of her immortal *anodos*, or "rising," where during her birth she initially rises from the sea and emerges into the sky. As Aphrodite navigates and traverses the distance between the two separate realms, they become intermingled by the act of her emergence. Moreover, this primordial moment signifies the mediating function of the goddess, and thus the *anodos* becomes central to her divine meaning and power. Here in the gap between sea and sky is the perpetual *mixis* or "mingling" that Aphrodite inspires and enjoys, and over which she holds sway. The *anodos* of Aphrodite exemplifies contact, blending and unity.

The Greek poet Hesiod, as we have seen, was the first to describe the primeval *anodos* of Aphrodite in his cosmogonic poem the *Theogony*, composed sometime in the eighth or seventh century BC. The Hesiodic narrative of Aphrodite's birth closely connects the two spheres of sea and sky, as the goddess rises from the sea into the upper air and first approaches the island of Cythera, and ultimately comes ashore on the sacred island of Cyprus (*Theogony* 188–206). Exposed to the bright blue sky and surrounded by deep water, the island itself represents the halfway point between sea and sky, as it marks out the consecrated liminal space in between the two realms where Aphrodite dwells. In blissful response to the union of sea and sky that the *anodos* of the goddess symbolizes, the sandy soil of Cyprus sends up shoots of grass as her divine feet touch land (*Theogony* 194–95). As Hesiod illustrates the scene, the *anodos* of the goddess immediately follows the castration of the sky god Ouranos.

> The genitalia themselves, freshly cut with flint, were thrown
> Clear of the mainland into the restless, white-capped sea,
> Where they floated a long time. A white foam from the god-flesh
> Collected around them, and in that foam a maiden developed
> And grew. Her first approach to land was near holy Kythera
> And from there she floated on to the island of Kypros.
> There she came ashore, an awesome, beautiful divinity.
> Tender grass sprouted up under her slender feet.
>
> (*Theogony* 188–95, trans. Lombardo, 1993)

Other Greek writers were likewise captivated by the concept of Aphrodite's *anodos*, and strove to articulate the extraordinary image of a goddess who shares in the realms of both sea and sky. The playwright Euripides explores the awesome and wide-ranging force of Aphrodite in his tragedy *Hippolytus*, produced in Athens in 428 BC. In an early scene, Phaedra's nurse desperately tries to encourage her lovesick mistress to alleviate her painful desire by making erotic overtures to her stepson, the sober youth Hippolytus. Driven by her maternal concern for Phaedra, the nurse warns her not to deny Aphrodite's irresistible power, or suffer her devastating retribution. The nurse's words encapsulate the comprehensive nature of Aphrodite's divine influence, which extends inexorably from sky to sea and encompasses everything in-between.

> "The goddess
> Cypris has the power of a flood tide;
> she's overwhelming. Those who yield to her

she will pursue more calmly; those who scorn her
or those who are unusually proud –
you can't imagine how she crushes them.

"Cypris wanders through the upper air;
she is in the ocean wave. All things on earth
come from her, the sower of desire,
whose children we all are."

(*Hippolytus* 443–50, trans. Svarlien, 2007)

The *anodos* of Aphrodite also captured the imaginations of ancient Greek artists. One of the most magnificent artistic representations of Aphrodite *Anadyomenē*, "Rising from the Sea," to survive from Greek antiquity is on the so-called Ludovisi throne, dated to around 480–460 BC: this large block of white marble, which probably formed part of a large altar, is carved with bas-reliefs in the late archaic or early classical style. Though the purpose, meaning and provenience of this puzzling monument have long been the subject of debate, most scholars now agree that the Ludovisi throne was originally part of an Ionic temple to Aphrodite (built *ca.* 480 BC) at the western Greek site of Locri Epizefiri in southern Italy (descriptive summary of the Ludovisi throne in Rosenzweig 2004). The Ludovisi throne can now be visited at the Museo Nazionale located at the charming Palazzo Altemps in the center of the city of Rome. On the main panel of the monument is a depiction of the birth of Aphrodite just as she is emerging from the water. The sculptor skilfully portrayed the goddess wearing a diaphanous garment, drenched with seawater, the thin fabric clinging to her upturned breasts and tracing the shape of her navel; she has a fillet or band tied around her head, and her long hair hangs heavy and wet on her neck and left shoulder as she lifts her face upwards to the right. With both of her arms outstretched, Aphrodite reaches up to two female attendants on either side of her, who are both clothed in long, see-through tunics and standing barefoot on the rocky shore. The two handmaidens, most likely either the Hours or Graces, grasp the newly born Aphrodite delicately under her arms to lift her up from the water, as they jointly raise a mantle or veil in front of the goddess, covering her from the waist down, in preparation to clothe her dripping body. With its play of upward-rising curves and overlapping drapery, the main panel of the Ludovisi throne is an exquisite rendering in marble of the very moment of Aphrodite's immortal *anodos*, or "rising." It is a symbol of the blending of sea and sky that belongs uniquely to Aphrodite.

Figure 6.1 Birth of Aphrodite. Relief on Ludovisi throne. *ca.* 480–460 BC. The Art Archive/ Museo Nazionale Terme Rome/Gianni Dagli Orti.

SEA AND SAILING

The *anodos* of Aphrodite begins in the sea. As the location of her original epiphany, and thus her sacred birthplace, the sea remains a fundamental site for many of Aphrodite's mythological, literary, artistic and cultic associations in ancient Greece. In contrast to Poseidon, the great Olympian god of the ocean, whose myths portray an irritable and unpredictable deity prone to causing deadly storms and tsunamis, Aphrodite's influence over their shared sphere mirrors her own tranquil emergence from the sea foam into the bright upper air: with a touch, she soothes the roiling waves and gentles the gusty winds. While Aphrodite's kinship with the sea reflects her aquatic genesis and her profound elemental power, it is also another expression of her close relationships with mortals, as she shows her concern for and involvement with humans who live near the shore or ply the waterways to make a living.

Aphrodite enjoyed many cult epithets in antiquity that reflect her marine origins and her intimate affinity with the sea (for a thorough survey of Aphrodite's marine cult titles: Pirenne-Delforge 1994). The goddess was known as Aphrodite *Pontia*, "She of the Deep Sea" (Pausanias, *Description of Greece* 2.34.11), and she was called *Pelagia*, "She of the Open Sea" (Artemidorus, *Interpretation of Dreams* 2.37); the names *Thalassaiē*, "She of the Sea," and *Galēnaiē*, "She of the Calm Sea," are also attested as cult titles (Pirenne-Delforge 1994). Like many maritime cultures throughout history, the ancient Greeks had numerous words for the saltwater realm, including the most common word for "the sea," *thalassa*, but also *pontos*, "the deep sea," and *pelagos*, "the open sea." Other noteworthy aquatic epithets demonstrate Aphrodite's close relationship with sailors and seafaring, merging her two foremost dominions over the waters of the sea and the breezes of the sky. As the goddess who promises successful navigation and safe voyages home, Aphrodite also enjoyed the cult epithets *Euploia*, "She of the Smooth Sailing" (Pausanias, *Description of Greece* 1.1.3); and *Limenia* or *Epilimenia*, "She of/at the Harbor" (Pausanias, *Description of Greece* 2.34.11). The sanctuary of Aphrodite *Euploia* at Knidos boasted the famous nude statue of the goddess sculpted by Praxiteles (*ca.* 350 BC), a site that became a major tourist attraction in later Greek and Roman antiquity.

Aphrodite was regularly worshipped at numerous ancient sanctuaries on beaches, islands and harbor towns, and in particular along the major trade routes used by Greek and Phoenician merchants and mariners, who played a significant role in the spread of her worship (most recently, with comprehensive overview: Larson 2007). Indeed, it was a frequent and expected structural element of Greek seaports and shorelines to feature a temple of Aphrodite, whose patrons would include ships' crews, sailors and marines, ship owners, traders, fishermen, recent immigrants and colonists, seagoing tourists and all the other salty types who might congregate on the waterfront. Situated on the water's edge in between land and sea, the beach or harbor represents a liminal location where the water meets the land and they converge, forming an altogether distinctive maritime milieu. So it was only natural to locate a temple or sanctuary of Aphrodite, goddess of *mixis*, in this interstitial space open to sea and sky. Such a coastal site was commemorated in a verse by Anyte of Tegea, an Arcadian Greek poet who lived in the early third century BC and was celebrated for her delicate epigrams. One of her surviving short poems describes a cult statue of Aphrodite located by the sea.

Kypris keeps this spot.
She loves to be here,
Always looking out
From the land over
The brilliant sea. She
Brings the sailors good
Voyage, and the sea
Quivers in awe of
Her gleaming image.

(poem 22, *Greek Anthology* 9.144, trans. Rexroth, 1999)

In this striking epigram, the poet Anyte blurs the spatial boundaries between the goddess perched high atop a bluff and the sea from which she was born and over which she still holds sway. Aphrodite gazes with benevolent delight and satisfaction over the shimmering expanse of ocean, no doubt admiring the reflection of her lovely figure rippling in the translucent water. Beyond the marina are the sailors in their ships at sea, full of gratitude for Aphrodite's divine blessing, and seeking to catch a glimpse of her kindly, smiling statue as a sign of their successful navigation. The last line of the epigram depicts the sea itself returning the goddess' gaze: beholding her shining, sunlit image, the waves tremble both with reverential wonder at her awesome power and with a *frisson* of pleasure at her radiant beauty. As their sight lines mingle through the bright air, the goddess and the sea join in mutual admiration of each other.

All along the Mediterranean coastline, cult sites consecrated to Aphrodite can be found wherever the ancient Greeks wandered and traveled by sea (for a complete review of Aphrodite's numerous cults organized by region: Pirenne-Delforge 1994). Her two most important islands are Cythera, where according to the Hesiodic birth story she first touched land, and Cyprus, her main cult site and permanent dwelling (*Theogony* 188–206). On Cyprus, scholars have identified hundreds of sanctuaries to Aphrodite dotted all over the island (most recently, on the primacy of Cyprus as the island of Aphrodite: Karageorghis 2005; Ulbrich 2008). The ancient capital of Paphos on Cyprus was the traditional spot where the newly born Aphrodite came ashore from the sea, and it was the location of her most important cult sanctuary and temple: Paphos is cited by Homer as the site of her sacred precinct and altar (*Odyssey* 8.362–63; note too Homeric hymn 5.58–59). In her marine aspect, the goddess also maintained associations with other islands and seaside locations. Aphrodite has mythological and cultic connections to Rhodes, an island in the eastern Aegean directly south of Knidos in Asia Minor. One version of the island's origins describes the union of Helios, the sun, with the eponymous sea nymph Rhode, who is called the "sea-child of Aphrodite" (Pindar, *Olympian* 7.13–14). The name of the island evokes Aphrodite's flower, the rose or *rhodon*, an image of which graced the island's coinage; and there was a major temple to Aphrodite dating to the third century BC in the ancient capital city.

The island of Crete was also an early center for the worship of Aphrodite, where she may have been associated with the cult of the Minoan goddess-princess Ariadne (Boedeker 1974). A connection between Aphrodite and Crete is suggested by the poet Sappho, who composed beautiful songs on the island of Lesbos around 600 BC, in a fragmentary *kletic* hymn addressed to the goddess. Sappho evokes a sensual mood as she summons Aphrodite from Crete to join her in a place of exquisite natural beauty, where the goddess' sanctuary is full of her symbolic attributes and favorite things: apples, roses and garlands of spring flowers, and sweetly scented air.

> Come to me here from Crete, to this holy
> temple where you have a delightful grove
> of apple trees, and altars fragrant
> with smoke of incense.
>
> Here cold water babbles through apple
> branches, and roses keep the whole place
> in shadow, and from the quivering leaves
> a trance of slumber falls;
>
> here a meadow, where horses pasture, blooms
> with flowers of spring, and the breezes
> gently blow . . .

In this place, Kypris, take up garlands,
and gracefully, in golden cups,
pour out nectar that has been mingled
with celebration . . .

(fragment 2.1–16, trans. Miller, 1996)

Aphrodite's aspect as a protector of mariners and merchants was especially strong in the Greek city of Naukratis in Egypt, which was located on the western branch of the Nile river, and served as the most important Egyptian harbor until the rise of nearby Alexandria later in antiquity. Naukratis was the first permanent Greek settlement in Egypt and functioned as a point of cultural and commercial exchange between the Greeks and Egyptians: the city's Greek name indicates Naukratis derived its "power from ships," and for much of its history, Naukratis was indeed a major trading emporium and a busy mercantile link between east and west. One of the most ancient structures in Naukratis is a temple in the sanctuary of Aphrodite, established most likely around 600 BC by traders and travelers of eastern Greek heritage (most recently, on Aphrodite and Naukratis: Larson 2007). The Greek historian Herodotus notes that the prostitutes of Naukratis were exceptionally alluring and thus quite successful in their business; he singles out one in particular, a Thracian freedwoman named Rhodopis, a famous courtesan who was the mistress of Charaxos, the brother of the poet Sappho (*The Histories* 2.135). With the constant bustle of visitors and merchants, and the quick availability of currency, the port city of Naukratis would have been a prime location for courtesans and prostitutes to set up shop; and the proximity of Aphrodite's temple in the city would have allowed them easy access to venerate their patron goddess.

The religious prominence of Aphrodite to the denizens of this trading port is revealed in a delightful story told by the native writer, Athenaeus of Naukratis (*ca.* the end of the second century AD), about the Greek merchant Herostratos, who worked the trade route between Paphos on Cyprus and Naukratis (*Deipnosophistai* 15.675f–76c). On his last stop in Paphos, Herostratos bought a small statue of Aphrodite for good luck and then set sail for Egypt. But the sea voyage south was beset by severe storms, and so, as Athenaeus tells it, Herostratos and the crew prayed to Aphrodite for their safe return. Suddenly, myrtle flowers began to bloom around the statuette and the ship was filled with a beautiful fragrance, signifying the benevolent presence of the goddess. Soon after the ship put into port at Naukratis unscathed, Herostratos dedicated the little statue in Aphrodite's sanctuary and furnished garlands of myrtle to all her worshippers. While Aphrodite's maritime aspect clearly represents her affinity for the sea and the pleasure she takes in the space between boundaries, it also confirms her capacity to intervene in the mortal realm and her special compassion for seafaring humans.

Aphrodite also had an influential presence in the ports that served Athens, the most important Greek *polis* in antiquity. Before the fifth century, the Athenians used the Bay of Phaleron as their harbor, and it was from here that the hero Theseus departed on his great sea journey to Crete (Pausanias, *Description of Greece* 1.1.2). Legend has it that Theseus sacrificed a female goat to Aphrodite on the shore before he set sail, to gain her favor and protection (Plutarch, *Life of Theseus* 18.2). Indeed, the goddess would have been an appropriate ally for the hero, both to ensure a safe sea voyage, and to facilitate his love affair with Ariadne, the princess of Crete. In the fifth century BC, the port of Athens was moved from Phaleron to Piraeus. During his archonship in 493 BC, the Athenian general Themistocles began to develop the waterfront of Piraeus, which was to serve as the main harbor of Athens and the home of the Athenian navy, starting in 477 BC after the war with Persia. Citing inscriptional evidence, scholars note that Themistocles seems to have dedicated an *Aphrodision*, a sanctuary to Aphrodite, at Piraeus after the battle of Salamis in 480 BC; remains of the temple have been found on the promontory at Eetioneia on the north side of Piraeus (most recently, on Aphrodite in the Piraeus: Rosenzweig 2004). Years later, according to the ancient sources, the Athenian general Konon also built a sanctuary to Aphrodite *Euploia* at Piraeus in celebration of his glorious naval victory over the Spartan fleet off the coast of Knidos in 394 BC (Pausanias, *Description of Greece* 1.1.3): whether Konon expanded the original Themistoclean sanctuary or built a distinct one is unclear. However, it is notable that this maritime Aphrodite, protector of seafarers, who was early on connected with the heroic cult of Theseus at Athens, was later associated with the entire Athenian navy and their victorious sea battles. Starting in the mid-fifth century BC, numerous Athenian vase paintings depict the *anodos* of Aphrodite embellished with vigorous nautical imagery – such as dolphins, swans, cockle shells and sails – emphasizing her affiliation with the sea, and by extension, the Athenian naval enterprise. Thus, since the Athenian fleet was a manifestation of the political authority of the *dēmos*, or the people, Aphrodite's benevolent bond with the sailors on the triremes would have also expressed her public aspect, her familiarity with humans, and her divine approval of Athenian democracy.

In the literary and artistic iconography of marine Aphrodite, the goddess is sometimes depicted accompanied by an aquatic *thiasos*, or a raucous group of ocean-dwelling followers. Like her principal earthly entourage, the Graces and the Hours, who are beautiful minor goddesses in their own right, nautical Aphrodite is often shown attended by the ubiquitous female sea deities, the Nereids (see Pausanias, *Description of Greece* 2.1.8; on the Nereids as Aphrodite's attendants in the post-Homeric texts: Larson 2001). The daughters of Nereus, an ancient Greek sea god, are salt-water nymphs who dwell in the sea: Hesiod succeeds in naming all fifty of them (*Theogony* 240–64). The Nereids are typically portrayed as lovely, lithe young women, occasionally depicted as mermaids, half-female and half-fish, who sing, dance, play musical instruments and ride the ocean waves on the backs of dolphins and other sea creatures. Like Aphrodite, the Nereids are kind and helpful to humans who cross the sea, and they assist sailors and travelers whenever they are in distress. Sailors believed the Nereids could prevent disasters at sea, so there are numerous altars and thank-offerings dedicated to the Nereids as a group on the islands, beaches, and at the mouths of rivers where they were mainly worshipped. With their shared commonality of purpose to protect seafarers and calm the waters, it is not surprising the Nereids appear as Aphrodite's main marine entourage in ancient Greek art and literature.

A perfect convergence of subject matter, imagery and song comes in a fragment of a poem of Sappho, where she prays to maritime Aphrodite and her sea-nymph companions, the Nereids, for the safe journey home of her wandering brother Charaxos. Perhaps he was returning home from his voyage to the Greek colony of Naukratis in Egypt, where he had spent time dallying with the notorious courtesan Rhodopis, much to his sister's disapproval (as reported by Herodotus, *The Histories* 2.135).

Kypris and you Nereids, grant
that my brother arrive here unharmed
and that everything his heart wishes
be perfectly achieved.

(fragment 5.1–4, trans. Miller, 1996)

To enhance her nautical aspect even further, the artistic iconography of aquatic Aphrodite is embellished with several marine attributes and creatures. One of the more frequent figurative attributes of sea deities in general is the dolphin, a creature that the ancient Greeks portrayed in numerous myths of the sea as friendly, intelligent and helpful to humans, thereby sharing the kindliness feature characteristic of the Nereids. Dolphins are commonly found in ancient Greek vase paintings of marine scenes, usually shown frisking alongside sea nymphs or gods. Although primarily sacred to Apollo as the god of the oracle at Delphi, the dolphin is sometimes depicted with marine Aphrodite in artistic representations, including vase paintings and small terracotta figurines; the dolphin may also appear as an element of the statue support in the larger sculptural versions of the Aphrodite *Anadyomenē*, "Rising from the Sea," image types that become popular in later Greek antiquity (Havelock 1995). Aphrodite in her marine aspect is often associated with the cockle shell, as in the illustration of her *anodos* on an Attic red-figure *pelikē* (*ca.* 370–360 BC), where the goddess is shown emerging from the sea in the heart of a shiny white scallop shell, accompanied by swimming fish and Eros fluttering overhead, and observed by Poseidon holding his trident. The ancient artistic motif of the goddess' *anodos* on a shell clearly influenced the most famous modern representation of Aphrodite's emergence from the sea: Sandro Botticelli's painting *The Birth of Venus* (*ca.* 1485), now housed in the Uffizi gallery in Florence. Aphrodite's iconographic link with the cockle shell has strong sexual overtones, since the half-opened bivalve shell visually evokes the female genitalia; even today, marine mollusks, shellfish and, in particular, oysters are still considered to possess powerful "aphrodisiac" properties. From the moment of her birth from the sea, Aphrodite's affinity with the saltwater realm offers an exceptionally potent network of symbols, meanings and functions.

SKY

After she rises from the sea, Aphrodite emerges into the bright upper air of the heavens, suggesting the goddess has a celestial aspect as well. As discussed earlier, the epithet *Ourania*, "Heavenly," is the most frequently attested and widespread cult title for Aphrodite throughout the ancient Greek world (most recently: Rosenzweig 2004). The ancient sources observe that Aphrodite was venerated as *Ourania* at her oldest and most sacred cult sanctuaries on Greek soil, while they also associate the title with the ancient Phoenicians, who were said to have introduced her cult to the Greeks (Herodotus, *The Histories* 1.105; Pausanias, *Description of Greece* 1.14.7). So some modern scholars interpret Aphrodite's cult title *Ourania* as an apparent link to the ancient Near Eastern love goddesses (e.g. Breitenberger 2006). Yet other scholars argue the epithet *Ourania* is essentially patronymic in nature, noting that the name clearly stems from Aphrodite's filial relationship to Ouranos, the primordial sky, as recounted in the Hesiodic narrative of her birth

Figure 6.2 Aphrodite in a seashell. Terracotta statuette, *ca.* fourth century BC. The Art Archive/National Archaeological Museum Athens/Gianni Dagli Orti.

(*Theogony* 188–206); the epithet "Heavenly" would also imply a fundamental affinity with the Indo-European sky god Zeus, who is named as Aphrodite's father in the Homeric epics (e.g. at *Iliad* 3.374) (Friedrich 1978). Thus, in each of the two principal ancient myths of her origins, Aphrodite maintains a direct and elemental bond to the sky as both her birthplace and the source of her paternity.

Another scholarly line of thinking claims that the celestial aspect implied by Aphrodite's cult title *Ourania* originates from her link to an early Indo-European Dawn goddess, who later developed into the Greek goddess of the dawn, Eos (Boedeker 1974). In this scenario, the ancient Greeks living in coastal areas and islands would have watched the sun rise in the east over the Aegean Sea, and so they would have formed an association between the dawn and the sea; later, they connected the early Indo-European dawn deity with Aphrodite's mythological *anodos* from the salt waters. Aphrodite would then represent the celestial deity who arose from the sea at daybreak, thereby agreeing with her main birth story. According to this argument, evidence for Aphrodite's original celestial nature can readily be found in the early Greek texts chiefly in her frequent epithet *dia* "bright" (e.g. *Iliad* 5.370); also in her association to clouds and fog (such as the mist around Paris, *Iliad* 3.381); and, most notably, in her connection to chariots, the traditional conveyances of celestial deities. However, in ancient Greek art and literature, numerous Greek deities are depicted in chariots that convey them through the sky: but it is noteworthy that the iconography of Aphrodite's chariot and its draft team can be quite distinctive. For example, in ancient Greek vase paintings, Aphrodite is often portrayed in a chariot drawn by horses, birds or winged Eros figures; for example, an Attic red-figure *amphora*, illustrating a gigantomachy (*ca.* 400–390 BC), shows the goddess driving a chariot of powerful horses while Ares, god of war, stands next to her in the cart and spears a giant. In book 5 of Homer's *Iliad*, after Aphrodite is wounded on the Trojan battlefield by the Greek hero Diomedes, the goddess asks Ares to lend her his chariot to escape through the sky.

> Ares gave her the gold-frontleted horses.
> She mounted the chariot gingerly,
> And Iris stepped in and took the reins.
> She cracked the whip and the team flew off
> And came in no time to steep Olympus,
> The gods' homestead.
>
> (*Iliad* 5.363–67, trans. Lombardo, 1997)

In the imaginations of the ancient Greeks, Aphrodite *Ourania* is connected to other celestial phenomena as well. The presence of wind or clouds often indicates her divine epiphany is about to occur. In the birth narrative of the sixth Homeric hymn, Aphrodite is wafted to the island of Cyprus by "the wet-gushing west wind" or *Zephyros* (hymn 6.3, trans. Ruden, 2005). After preparing herself to seduce Anchises in the fifth Homeric hymn, Aphrodite heads straight to Troy: "High in the clouds she made a speedy journey" (hymn 5.67, trans. Ruden, 2005). The western Greek poet, Ibycus (*ca.* second half of the sixth century BC), describes the onset of erotic desire as "like the Thracian north wind ablaze with lightning, rushing from Aphrodite" (fragment 286.8–10, trans. Miller, 1996). During later Greek antiquity, Aphrodite is associated with the planet Venus, the brightest object visible in the sky after the sun and the moon (Heimpel 1982). The planet Venus was also known as *Eosphoros*, the "morning star," or *Hesperos*, the "evening star," since the Greeks recognized that this dazzling celestial body was very close to the orbit of the sun and shone brightest at those in-between moments just before nightfall or just before sunrise (see Plato, *Timaeus* 38d; *Laws* 821c). Both dusk and dawn have erotic connotations, as the time when lovers meet or separate, and thus are sacred to Aphrodite, who inspires the day and night to mingle at these liminal moments in a kind of cosmological *mixis*. Such an erotic transition is evoked in an anonymous Greek epigram, most likely dating from the Hellenistic period (third or second century BC).

> Awake all night till the
> Beautiful morning star,
> Leontion lay, taking
> Her full of golden Sthenios.
> Now she offers to Kypris
> The lyre she played with the
> Muses, all through the long night,
> On that night-long festival.
>
> (poem 5, *Greek Anthology* 5.201, trans. Rexroth, 1999)

After a night-long celebration of joyful song and sexual pleasure, the appearance in the sky of the radiant morning star at dawn signals the moment when the sated lovers must part, and perhaps promise each other to meet again. To ensure such an outcome, the musician, Leontion, dedicates her instrument in a shrine of Aphrodite, no doubt hoping the goddess will show her divine favor once more with the arrival of twilight.

Mountains

As the goddess whose influence touches the sky, the goddess Aphrodite is also associated with mountains, most notably Mt. Ida in Troy, Acrocorinth in the Greek city of Corinth and Mt. Eryx on the island of Sicily (on Aphrodite and mountains: Friedrich 1978). In Greek mythology, literature and cult, the mountain peak is considered a hallowed location interstitial between land and sky. The Greek gods dwell in immortal bliss on mountain tops, in particular upon Mt. Olympus, high above the world and shrouded in mist, but still close enough to approach the earthly realm and interfere in the lives of humans. The mountain summit is often portrayed in Greek myths as the sacred place of cross-boundary *mixis*, where gods and mortals meet, communicate and mingle. Thus, Aphrodite's close connection with the peaks of mountains reflects a key aspect of her religious meaning, the urge towards *mixis*, while her divine epiphanies upon mountain pinnacles play an important role in some of her most noteworthy myths. One of her cult epithets at her sanctuary at Knidos was Aphrodite *Akraia*, "She of the Peak," or "High Point," which may refer to the fact that her famous cult statue was placed high upon a bluff or promontory overlooking the sea (Pausanias, *Description of Greece* 1.1.3). But the title may also imply Aphrodite's intimate affinity for the pure, intoxicating air of the mountain heights.

The ancient Greek writers recount how Aphrodite had a particular affection for the peak of Mt. Ida in Troy, a highly erotically charged location in a land famous for its sexually attractive and thrill-seeking males. It was here on Mt. Ida that the epic poets say the celebrated Judgment of Paris took place, when the Trojan prince awarded Aphrodite first prize in the divine beauty contest and thereafter became one of the goddess' favorites (*Cypria* fragment 1). According to Homer, the goddess Hera, with Aphrodite's magical help, seduces her husband, the great god Zeus, upon the dewy grass along the slopes of Mt. Ida, in the famous *Dios Apatē* episode (*Iliad* 14.153–351). Aphrodite also finds the lofty location of Mt. Ida irresistible for a sexual rendezvous, as recorded in the earliest Greek sources (Hesiod, *Theogony* 1008–10; Homer, *Iliad* 2.819–21). As the full story unfolds in the fifth Homeric hymn, when the goddess sees the handsome Trojan cattleman Anchises herding cows "among the many springs of Ida's tall peaks" (hymn 5.54, trans. Ruden, 2005), she immediately incurs a powerful desire to sleep with him. After she bathes, dresses and perfumes herself at her shrine at Paphos on the island of Cyprus (hymn 5.58–66), Aphrodite swoops through the bright upper air down to the craggy folds of Mt. Ida to seduce Anchises in his cozy mountain cabin.

> High in the clouds she made a speedy journey
> To Ida, rich in springs, mother of wild things,
> And walked across the mountain to the shelter.
> A rush of bears and fast, deer-gobbling leopards,
> Gray wolves, and bright-eyed lions fawned around her.
> She had a look at these and found them charming.
> She tossed some lust to make the whole assortment
> Pair off and do it in the shadowy coverts.
>
> (hymn 5.67–74, trans. Ruden, 2005)

Aphrodite's own intense erotic desire for Anchises spills over into the local environment, as she cheerfully inspires the ferocious predators, now fawning and frisky, to couple in the dappled mountain thickets. Some scholars see Aphrodite's influence over the wild beasts in this passage as evidence that she is identified here with the Asiatic Great mother figure, or Cybele, who was worshipped on Mt. Ida in ancient times (Smith 1981; Breitenberger 2007); while other scholars argue, rather more persuasively, that Aphrodite's control over the animals in these verses of the hymn suggests a possible link to the generalized powers of the love goddess in the Near East, who is often portrayed as having sway over animals and their reproduction (Budin 2003; Faulkner 2008). Most significantly, the depiction of Aphrodite here as a "mistress of beasts" highlights her close affinity for the untamed mountain milieu she has just entered for the purpose of a sexual seduction. Indeed, it is Mt. Ida that is called the "mother of wild things" (hymn 5.68), as the mountain in Greek literature and mythology is the traditional domain of predatory beasts: so Aphrodite's animal-taming aspect here is most likely associated primarily with her own heightened sexual drive as she arrives on Mt. Ida.

High above the ancient city of Corinth, an important commercial center in antiquity, loomed the huge monolithic rock known as Acrocorinth, or "Upper Corinth," the fortified acropolis of the city. According to the ancient sources, the Corinthians believed a prehistoric dispute between Poseidon, the god of the sea, and Helios, the sun, divided their territory. After the conflict, Poseidon took possession of the Isthmus, while Helios assumed control of Acrocorinth, thereby separating the busy waterways from the high mountain (Pausanias, *Description of Greece* 2.1.6). Later, according to the legend, Helios granted Acrocorinth to the goddess Aphrodite, to serve as her own sacred ground (Pausanias, *Description of Greece* 2.4.6). During the classical period, there was a major temple to Aphrodite on the summit of Acrocorinth (on the influential cult of Aphrodite at Corinth: Pirenne-Delforge 1994). At a much later date, the travel writer Pausanias (second century AD) described the shrine of the goddess there, saying it was decorated with images depicting Helios, Eros holding a bow, and an "armed" *hoplismenē* statue of Aphrodite (*Description of Greece* 2.5.1). Although the notorious ancient anecdote (recorded in Strabo, *Geography* 8.6.20) regarding the practice of "sacred prostitution" in service to Aphrodite at Corinth may be discounted as an historiographic myth (most recently: Budin 2008), no doubt the goddess was indeed venerated on Acrocorinth by the local courtesans, as well as by the various traders, sailors and tourists who passed through the bustling, mercantile city.

In Sicily, the mountain site sacred to the goddess Aphrodite was at Mt. Eryx on the wooded northwest shoulder of the island. Evidence suggests Aphrodite may have taken over a shrine here from the Near Eastern goddess, Astarte, when the Greeks took over the region from the

Phoenicians (on the cult: Pirenne-Delforge 1994). The ancient sources note that the shrine of Aphrodite *Erycinē* on Mt. Eryx dated to remotest antiquity, and it was also described as a very wealthy sanctuary, rivaling the shrine at Paphos on Cyprus in riches (Pausanias, *Description of Greece* 8.24.6). In the mythological tradition, Aphrodite rescued Boutes, one of the Argonauts, when he was entranced by the Sirens' singing and threw himself off the ship; the goddess fell in love with him and took him to Lilybaion on the west coast of Sicily, where he became king (Apollodorus, *The Library* 1.9.25). The Greek historian, Diodorus of Sicily (*ca.* first century BC), notes that the son of Aphrodite and Boutes was Eryx, who built a striking shrine and temple to Aphrodite on the highest point of the mountain, and dedicated a cult there to Aphrodite *Erycinē* (*The Library of History* 4.83); however, the Roman epic poet Vergil says that Aphrodite's Trojan son, Aeneas, built the temple on Mt. Eryx on his way to Italy (*Aeneid* 5.759–60). Roman historical sources suggest that the worship of Aphrodite *Erycinē* was introduced from Sicily into Rome, where she was worshipped as Venus Erycina, around the time of the Second Punic War (*ca.* 200 BC) (Livy, *History of Rome* 22.9, 10; 23.30). If so, then the sanctuary at Mt. Eryx would be an incredibly significant point of contact and transition for Aphrodite's assumption into the wider Roman religious context.

Birds

Since they inhabit the sky and soar through the heavens with easy grace, birds have long been perceived as universal symbols of divine insight, epiphany and transformation (on the early religious significance of birds: Johnson 1994). Birds are ubiquitous throughout Greek mythology as the avian symbols of and companions to the gods. In ancient Greek art and literature, Aphrodite is often joined together with a variety of different birds that appear perched on her shoulders, in her lap or on her hands, fluttering around her head, or pulling her sky chariot. The most common birds associated with Aphrodite are doves, pigeons, sparrows and assorted waterfowl, including swans, geese and ducks: her birds are not typically predatory (Friedrich 1978). Aphrodite's ornithic symbols are chiefly related to her celestial and aquatic aspects, and, like the goddess herself, the birds function as intermediaries who easily cross boundaries between the heavenly and earthly realms. While Aphrodite's bird emblems clearly establish her affinity for the sky and sea, her birds are also strongly evocative of her dominion over love and sexuality, as the ancient Greeks considered birds to be erotic by nature. According to

Aristophanes, the Athenian comic playwright (*ca.* 448–385 BC), the race of birds was born from the union of Eros, god of sexual desire, and Chaos, the primordial spatial gap; thus, birds are of a far earlier generation than even the Olympian gods (*Birds* 685–707). In the comedy, the chorus leader of the birds proves their connection to the erotic sphere by explaining they are winged and quick like the god Eros, and they facilitate love affairs, since birds are offered as gift tokens of passion and can sway even the most recalcitrant of lovers. So there may be more than one term mediating between Aphrodite and her birds: not only the celestial and aquatic, but also the erotic.

Aphrodite's most significant and persistent bird symbol is the dove, an amiable bird that encompasses an intricate network of meanings and values: affection, harmony, peace, tranquility and love. The "lovey-dovey" behavior of these sweet-tempered birds, with their billing and cooing and apparent fondness for their mates, suggests an analogy to the foremost sphere of influence belonging to the goddess of love and sexuality. Some scholars interpret the pattern of Aphrodite's correlation with doves as a direct inheritance from the cults of the Near Eastern love goddesses, especially the Semitic Ishtar and the Phoenician Astarte (most recently: Breitenberger 2007). Other scholars observe that representations of bird and dove goddesses are attested elsewhere in the ancient Minoan-Mycenaean world (Friedrich 1978); however, the scant archaeological evidence does not actually support the presence of a dove goddess in the iconography of the Bronze Age Aegean. In fact, in extant early Greek literature, doves are not connected with Aphrodite, although doves are mentioned several times in the Homeric poems, usually in similes illustrating their timid nature (for example, of Artemis fleeing Hera: *Iliad* 21.493; of the serving women: *Odyssey* 22.468). With such a paucity of literary and archaeological evidence, it may be possible to surmise that Aphrodite's mythological association with doves developed its meaning independent of the bird symbolism linked to earlier goddesses.

By the sixth and fifth centuries BC, and later on into the Hellenistic period, the iconographic association of Aphrodite with doves as her essential avian motif becomes ubiquitous in Greek art and cult. In archaic and classical Greek vase painting, Aphrodite is frequently depicted accompanied by doves. On an archaic Attic red-figure *kylix*, attributed to the Oltos painter (*ca.* 515–510 BC), Aphrodite is portrayed holding a rather large dove in her hand, as she is seated next to Ares among the gods feasting. A late classical Apulian red-figure volute *kratēr*, most likely by the Ilioupersis painter (*ca.* 365–355 BC), shows Aphrodite with a small bird, presumably a dove or sparrow, on her lap. Another Apulian red-figure *skyphos*, perhaps from the same workshop as the *kratēr* (*ca*. 375–355 BC), shows Aphrodite with a small dove perched daintily on her finger. Doves regularly appear in the cultic iconography of Aphrodite's Athenian sanctuaries: doves are depicted with knotted fillets in their beaks decorating the dedicatory relief sculpture at the shrine of Aphrodite *Pandēmos* on the southwest slope of the Acropolis; also, votive offerings in the shape of small doves carved of white marble were found at Aphrodite's shrine at Daphni, about ten miles northwest of Athens (Rosenzweig 2004). An Attic inscription from the Hellenistic period (dated to 283–282 BC) refers to an official offering of a dove or pigeon to purify the sanctuary of Aphrodite *Pandēmos* (Breitenberger 2007). In the Greek artistic and cultic record, at least, doves are Aphrodite's bird emblem par excellence.

The most well-known literary reference to Aphrodite and birds comes in one of the most celebrated poems from Greek antiquity: Sappho's *kletic* hymn summoning her patron goddess (poem 1). Sappho portrays Aphrodite arriving from heaven on a chariot drawn by sparrows. The ancient Greeks considered sparrows noteworthy for their sexual promiscuity and fecundity, not unlike rabbits to the modern consciousness, and thus they would be suitable draft birds for the goddess of love and sexuality. Moreover, these speedy, social, highly motivated birds are also appropriate for Aphrodite's sudden and vigorous divine epiphany.

> Immortal Aphrodite on your richly crafted throne,
> daughter of Zeus, weaver of snares, I beg you,
> do not with sorrows and with pains subdue
> my heart, O Lady,
>
> but come to me, if ever at another time as well,
> hearing my voice from far away,
> you heeded it, and leaving your father's house
> of gold, you came,
>
> yoking your chariot. Graceful sparrows
> brought you swiftly over the black earth,
> with a thick whirring of wings, from heaven down
> through the middle air.
>
> (poem 1.1–12, trans. Miller, 1996)

Aphrodite is often associated with water birds, such as swans, geese and ducks. Representing the union of sea and sky, the iconography of Aphrodite and water birds combines both her celestial and aquatic aspects. Also, like the sparrows in Sappho's poem, Aphrodite's water birds are correlated with the goddess in flight to or from the heavens. In Greek art, Aphrodite is shown carried by a water bird, standing or sitting while riding on its back as if airborne, or with waterfowl drawing her chariot, soaring through the sky. The artistic image of the goddess borne through the air by water birds symbolizes her easy passage between the two realms. On the interior of a particularly beautiful white-ground *kylix* from Rhodes, attributed to the Pistoxenos painter (*ca.* 470–460 BC), Aphrodite is shown riding a giant goose, sitting elegantly side-saddle upon the flying bird. The graceful goddess wears a modest cap, or *sakkos*, on her head, a long red dress, and delicate sandals on her feet, while she holds a curling frond of a plant in one hand. Another representation of Aphrodite that evokes the modern image of "Mother Goose" is a terracotta statuette from Taranto (*ca.* 380 BC) depicting the goddess, together with a smaller-size Eros, sitting comfortably atop a large goose. Swans also appear as avian transport for Aphrodite, though sometimes it is quite difficult to tell swans from geese in Greek art. A lovely Attic red-figure *lekythos* shows the goddess, wearing a diadem and carrying a scepter, with her bare feet dangling, as she nestles on the back of a well-built swan with outspread wings, as if in flight. Another vase, a late classical Attic red-figure *pelikē* (*ca.* 350 BC), depicts Aphrodite standing on the back of a large white swan who appears to pull her through the waves, as indicated by the presence of a nearby dolphin. While swans are also associated with music and thus are sacred to the god Apollo, their ostensibly devoted behavior towards their partners, with whom they mate for life, suggests an affinity for the goddess of love. More notably, swans also have erotic connotations in Greek mythology, as in the tale of Zeus' taking on the powerful form of a swan to seduce Leda, mother of Helen, Aphrodite's favorite mortal woman.

OVERVIEW

Our exploration of Aphrodite's association to the sea and the sky reveals a goddess who represents the union of the two realms in an elemental *mixis*, or "mingling." Aphrodite's *anodos* rising from the sea into the sky embodies the blurring of spatial boundaries that the goddess always seeks to inspire. We have seen how the goddess exhibits both marine and celestial attributes in ancient Greek art, literature, cult and mythology. In her aquatic aspect, Aphrodite enjoys numerous marine shrines, sanctuaries and epithets, while she protects and guides sailors and seafarers. Marine Aphrodite is often accompanied by Nereids, dolphins and other

Figure 6.3 Aphrodite riding a swan or goose. White-ground *kylíx*, Pistoxenos painter, *ca.* 470–460 BC. The Art Archive/HarperCollins Publishers.

sea creatures. As a goddess with influence over the heavens, Aphrodite is sometimes depicted in her celestial aspect, riding in chariots through the sky or connected with cosmological phenomena. Aphrodite's affinity for mountain peaks also implies her association with the pure upper air, as does her ubiquitous bird symbolism. Aphrodite's sway over the collective spheres of sea and sky expresses her wide-ranging power within the natural world.

APHRODITE
AFTERWARDS

7

AFTER GREEK ANTIQUITY

In this final chapter, we will consider Aphrodite's enduring power as a symbol of beauty, adornment, love and sexuality, an image that lasted beyond Greek antiquity and still persists today in modern popular culture. As background to this inquiry, we will first take a brief look at the intersection between Greek Aphrodite and Roman Venus, exploring how the representations of the two goddesses influenced each other for a time during Greco-Roman antiquity, and how the figure of the Roman goddess Venus subsequently came to dominate the Western literary and artistic tradition, especially in Europe. Next this chapter will investigate the various implications and functions of the brand name "Aphrodite" in contemporary marketing, beauty and fashion advertising, and book publishing. This chapter will conclude with a survey of some memorable on-screen appearances of Aphrodite in modern film and television productions.

APHRODITE AND VENUS

In the imaginations of the ancient Greek writers and artists, and in the religious cults and observances of worshippers throughout the wider Greek-speaking world, the goddess Aphrodite evokes a specific cluster of images and meanings. She is the embodiment of beauty and adornment, the impulse towards erotic *mixis*, and the ongoing contact between the elemental realms of sea and sky. During the later centuries of the Hellenistic period, however, the emergence of Rome as an important player on the Mediterranean scene introduced new manifestations and interpretations of the Greek goddess. Aphrodite was subsequently appropriated and, to some degree, remodeled by the Roman cultural and political machine.

The earliest Romans in all probability worshipped a Latin goddess named Venus, who was sometimes associated with vegetation, gardens and springtime, and who may have also incorporated aspects of the ancient Etruscan love goddess Turan (on the Roman worship of Venus: Schilling 1982). The oldest known Roman temple to Venus was built at Rome, most likely at the base of the Aventine Hill near the Circus Maximus, at the beginning of the third century BC: the temple had been vowed by Q. Fabius Maximus Gurges in 295 BC. This sanctuary was dedicated to Venus *Obsequens*, the "Indulgent" or "Compliant" goddess, who apparently was not yet associated with the Greek Aphrodite. Later, in the middle of the third century BC, the bilingual dramatist and epic poet Livius Andronicus (*ca.* 280–200 BC), who hailed from the Greco-Roman city of Tarentum in southern Italy, adapted Homer's *Odyssey* into Latin verse, an event of singular literary and cultural importance in the history of Roman letters. In the process of producing his translation, Livius Romanized the names and mythological personae of the Greek gods, and he seems to have either proposed, perpetuated or highlighted particular connections between pairs of Greek and Roman deities, including any existing links between the Greek Aphrodite and the Roman Venus. But according to Roman historical sources (Livy, *History of Rome* 22.9, 10; 23.30), the official religious integration of Venus and Aphrodite occurred at the end of the third century BC (*ca.* 200 BC), when the cult of Venus Erycina was introduced into Rome from the Sicilian sanctuary of Aphrodite at Mt. Eryx. Thus, by the beginning of the second century BC, the mythological, cultic and iconographical association between the Greek Aphrodite and the Roman Venus became more or less established and was consistently represented as such in native Roman drama, art and poetry.

From this auspicious connection between the two goddesses came the even more overtly valuable link between Venus/Aphrodite and the glamorous heroic past told in the cycle of Greek epic verse. The Romans soon began to appreciate the cultural and political benefits in having Venus as the foremother of their entire people: they considered her to be their direct ancestress through her son, the Trojan hero Aeneas, who had escaped the burning rubble of Troy and had come to Italy, where he settled the area that would later become the city of Rome. In this incarnation she was worshipped as Venus *Genetrix*, "Mother Venus," and was invested with a much more maternal aspect than she ever embodied as the Greek Aphrodite, who, as we have seen, was never an appreciably maternal or kourotrophic deity in the religious ideology of the early Greeks (Budin 2003). While Venus was worshipped by all Romans as their divine national mother, the goddess was particularly important and useful to the Roman general and dictator Julius Caesar (100–44 BC), who shrewdly traced the lineage of the Julian *gens*, his extended clan, directly back to Iulus, the son of Aeneas: in Latin, *Iulius* would be the eponymous family adjective from the proper name, Iulus. Julius Caesar frequently utilized this divine genealogy in his personal propaganda, and even dedicated a temple to Venus *Genetrix* in his new Forum Iulium during his triumph in 46 BC (Cassius Dio, *Roman History* 43.22.2). Later, Caesar's chosen heir, Augustus (63 BC – AD 14), as well as all the subsequent Julio-Claudian rulers of Rome, would regularly emphasize this politically advantageous natal connection of the imperial family to the goddess Venus.

One of the most significant literary appearances of the Greek-influenced figure of Venus comes in book 1 of the *Aeneid*, the celebrated national epic of Augustan Rome composed by Rome's great poet, Vergil (70–19 BC). In this programmatic scene, the goddess appears to her Trojan son, Aeneas, whose ships have just been blown by a storm to Carthage, but he has no clue where he is or what he should do. Disguised as a young huntress, Venus encourages him not to feel sorry for himself but to seek Queen Dido's goodwill to help him fulfill his duty and advance his destined path to Italy. As she leaves him, Venus allows her true identity, both divine and maternal, to show through her masquerade, much to the surprise and distress of the lonesome Aeneas. The scene is rife with iconographical elements and details derived from Greek literary and artistic sources, while at the same time it underscores the complicated relationship between this Roman goddess mother and her son, the great founding hero of Rome.

> She spoke, and as she turned, her neck
> Shone with roselight. An immortal fragrance
> From her ambrosial locks perfumed the air,
> Her robes flowed down to cover her feet,
> And every step revealed her divinity.
> Aeneas knew his own mother, and his voice
> Fell away from her as she disappeared:
>
> "You! Do you have to cheat your son
> With empty appearances? Why can't we
> At least embrace and talk to each other
> In our own true voices?"
>
> With this rebuke
> Aeneas turned toward the city.
> Venus, for her part, enclosed both her son

And his companion in a dark cloud,
Cloaking them in a mist so that none would see them
As they walked along and so detain them
With questions about their reasons for coming.
And then she was gone, aloft to Paphus,
Happy to see her temple again, where Arabian
Incense curls up from one hundred altars
And fresh wreaths of flowers sweeten the air.

(*Aeneid* 1.402–17, trans. Lombardo, 2005)

Such influence in mythological iconography may have worked both ways, as some evidence suggests that the image of the later Hellenistic Greek Aphrodite was also affected or even altered under the powerful and pervasive impact exerted by the Roman veneration of their national mother goddess. During the late Hellenistic period, when the Greeks were trying to determine how to respond to the growing political and military authority of Rome, some Greek cities seem to have manipulated their depiction of and affiliations to Aphrodite/Venus in order to win the diplomatic favor and protection of the increasingly dominant Romans (most recently, with excellent survey of evidence: Wallensten 2009). These Greek strategies included claiming ancestral connections to Trojan relatives of Aeneas or playing up their Trojan connections in general, thereby implying an ethnic or familial connection to the Trojan-descended Romans. Even more notably, in some Hellenistic Greek cities the representation of Aphrodite, along with the nature of her local religious cults, appears to have been modified, as certain Romanized elements become more pronounced. Specifically, within the context of Roman ascendancy, the later Hellenistic Greek Aphrodite appears to become more maternal and more militaristic in character, as well as more concerned with administrative bureaucracy, for example, in her role as a divine guardian of political magistrates. In short, Aphrodite becomes more Roman, as the Greeks of the later Hellenistic period astutely discovered the numerous political and diplomatic benefits inherent in likening their goddess to Venus, the divine mother of the new masters of the Mediterranean.

In the centuries following Greco-Roman antiquity, the image of Roman Venus dominates the literary and artistic scene, and Greek Aphrodite rarely appears in anything close to her original Hellenic incarnation. Although the name and image of "Aphrodite" could have been used as a potentially effective synonym for feminine beauty, love and eroticism, these concepts are nearly always symbolized by the figure of Roman Venus throughout the Western tradition, especially in Europe. The courtly love poets of medieval France composed verses that idealized the lady beloved as the goddess Venus, while the artists of the Italian Renaissance employed their mistresses, or those of their wealthy patrons, as models for allegorical portrayals of Venus in painting and sculpture. Although William Shakespeare (1564–1616) is most famous for his plays, the Elizabethan dramatist also wrote a long narrative poem *Venus and Adonis* (1593) that retells the myth of the goddess' intense love for the handsome youth. The English Romantic poets, such as John Keats (1795–1821) and Percy Bysshe Shelley (1792–1822), were well known for celebrating Hellenism in all its lyric forms, and yet their poems still refer to "Venus," just like the Roman writers did, as in these lines from Keats' poem, *Endymion* (1818): ". . . see her hovering feet/ More bluely vein'd, more soft, more whitely sweet/ Than those of sea-born Venus" (lines 624–26). Even the erotic novella *Venus in Furs* (1870) by Austrian author Leopold von Sacher-Masoch inspired American musician Lou Reed to write a pop song of the same name, *Venus in Furs* (1967), that appeared on the debut album of his band, the Velvet Underground. So, as this brief and subjective survey suggests, the dominant mythological iconography for representing the ancient goddess of love, sex and beauty, at least in the cultural history of the West, clearly emerged from the Latin literary and artistic tradition of Roman Venus rather than from Greek Aphrodite.

APHRODITE TODAY

Today, more than ever, Aphrodite is skilfully marketed as an appealing brand name. Perhaps because her name was largely excluded from the more canonical genres of Western art and literature, the name "Aphrodite" is bringing something new and fresh to current popular awareness: while the appellation "Venus" sounds old-fashioned and stodgy, like something out of a museum catalogue or a college textbook, the name "Aphrodite" sounds innovative, edgy and hip. The recent branding of the goddess' name and image as the epitome of contemporary charm and glamour evokes her most essential realms of divine influence: that is, the beautification and adornment of the face, hair and body for the purpose of erotic allure.

To discover where Aphrodite primarily resides in modern popular culture, we need only to look to the glitzy business of fashion and beauty advertising. Today, the name "Aphrodite" and the goddess' image are being used ubiquitously throughout the world to entice customers and clients to purchase beauty services, trends and products. There are several Aphrodite-brand beauty creams, lotions and scrubs, all of which highlight the use of natural and organic ingredients such as Greek olive oil, mountain herbs, and marine-based extracts like seaweed, algae and ocean salts. One line of Aphrodite-brand beauty products made on the island of Crete promises that its secret ancient formula has "stood the test of time." Aphrodite's name graces the entryways and web portals of every category of beauty service provider, including hair salons, laser treatment parlors, cosmetic enhancement and plastic surgery studios, beauty supply shops and skin care centers. Beauty entrepreneurs employ the name and likeness of Aphrodite in their advertising to announce their particular areas of expertise: one is a "bridal make-up specialist," another is a "beauty pageant consultant," while another organizes special-occasion "beauty-pampering parties."

One particularly slick modern collocation of Greek mythological figures locates "Aphrodite's Beauty Salon" right next to "Zeus' Gym" and describes the goddess' spot as "a place to relax away from the weights room." A famous European purveyor of fine beauty products maintains an exceptionally clever website urging its visitors to "Get the goddess look: Aphrodite," and offers an inventory of "Aphrodite-inspired products that will unleash the love goddess in you." Listing nearly all of Aphrodite's specific scents, colors and attributes, along with their relevant and mostly accurate mythological citations, this website promotes such items as "Shell" tinted face make-up, "myrtle and rose" scented cologne imbued with "the essence of the Mediterranean," nail polish in a tawny color called "Three Way Mirror," and creamy eye shadow in the hues "Dove," "Sparrow" and "Swan," that promise "true love-bird appeal." The shopping-list format presented on this website recalls the tendency towards catalog-like specificity in descriptions of Aphrodite's physical beauty in the earliest Greek texts (e.g. *Iliad* 3.396–98; *Odyssey* 8.362–66). Another popular and ultra-chic brand of nail polish recently introduced a shade dubbed "Aphrodite's Pink Nightie," no doubt relying on the amusing internal rhyming scheme as much as on the attractive blush color of the bottle and the sexually provocative reference to the goddess of love's lingerie.

At Aphrodite Image Consultancy, an international center for "image coaching," customers can sign up for personal sessions or corporate workshops to reach their fullest beauty and fashion potential, as they are lured with blandishments: "Be a Model! Be a Beauty Queen! Be a Flight Attendant!" This company's sumptuous advertising hinges explicitly on the popular image of Aphrodite as the divine embodiment of beauty that inspires love, while inviting prospective clients to achieve their own pragmatic level of success.

Aphrodite ("risen from sea-foam") is the Greek goddess of love and beauty. She is often described as a gorgeous, perfect and eternally young woman with a beautiful body. Her girdle had magical powers to compel love.

Maybe looks aren't everything. But beauty is a major obsession. In a world where we are bombarded by images of "perfect" looking celebrities, we are all in danger of feeling bad about how we look. Pressure to live up to unrealistic ideas can zap the fun out of fashion and beauty, and bring a nasty case of low self-esteem.

Here at Aphrodite image consultancy, we have the ability to help you get a grip on what's really going on, get creative with your personal style, and get in touch with your own idea of beauty. We have the skills to make you beautiful and with beauty, you will better command love in the form of respect and admiration.

(from www.aphrodite.com.sg)

In the world of fashion advertising and promotion, Aphrodite's name, likeness and mythological narratives are also frequently utilized to attract consumers. The name Aphrodite can be found in the designation and marketing of numerous fashion-related businesses, including apparel manufacturers, dry cleaners, ready-to-wear collections, clothing warehouses and distributors, jewelry designers, and of course in the names of retail boutiques, both online and on the street. Although Aphrodite is mainly associated with the women's fashion industry, even some menswear outlets incorporate her name in their store titles and marketing materials: perhaps the allusion to Aphrodite is intended to evoke the images of her handsome and presumably well-dressed male favorites in ancient Greek myth, such as Paris, Anchises and Adonis. One style-setting website called "Aphrodite's Fashion Show" encourages its members and guests to create and maintain fashion collages: these are individual photo collections of clothing, shoes, jewelry, hats, handbags and other trendy accessories grouped together to conjure up a particular fashion ambience. Again, the layering effect of the various tiered items of adornment recalls the literary portrayals of Aphrodite's own personal fashion inventory of clothing, jewelry and hair ornaments (especially as described in the Homeric hymns: hymn 5.58–66, 84–90; hymn 6.5–18). The website asserts it is for "stylish people," mainly females, as it claims, "unless some naughty gods decided to watch," which may be an unintentionally crudite reference to Aphrodite's exposure to the gaze of the male Olympians in the infamous tale of the bard Demodocus (*Odyssey* 8.266–369). Based on the color schemes, shapes and styles of the posted outfits, each is furnished with an explanatory tag line evocative of Aphrodite's role in Greek mythology, such as: "Mess with the Mortals," "Underworld Visit," "Skipping Hera's Party," "Welcome Persephone,"

"Poseidon's Beach Party," and the particularly attention-grabbing "Cleaning Up After Pandora." It is difficult to imagine the staid and matronly Roman Venus participating in anything like this kind of frivolous, fashionable fun.

Yet while Venus has dominated the traditional literary marketplace, Aphrodite is just now coming into her own in contemporary bookstores. The recent trend in marketing the name and image of Aphrodite is quickly spreading to the business of book publishing, where the simple evocation of the goddess' persuasive-sounding name offers a guarantee of profitable returns on any publication venture. Ever since the release of Isabel Allende's *Aphrodite: A Memoir of the Senses* (1998), there has been an upsurge in the use of the name "Aphrodite" to enhance the cover appeal of books in a variety of different subject fields. Interestingly enough, these volumes have little or nothing to do with Aphrodite herself, excluding, of course, academic books on the topics of ancient Greek religion, mythology and literature: rather, these non-classical works chiefly utilize the enticing name "Aphrodite" as a superficial jacket adornment to attract the customer to buy the book. Even Allende's volume, a lush 315-page meditation on the intersection of the culinary and sexual appetites, barely mentions Aphrodite, and only in connection with explaining the origin of the word "aphrodisiac."

> Marine mollusks and crustaceans are believed to have the highest aphrodisiac value, first among them, oysters. The word *aphrodisiac* comes from Aphrodite, the Greek goddess of love, born of the sea foam after Cronus castrated his father Uranus and threw the genitals into the deep – a rather unnatural means of fertilization, but in that case it worked well and the beautiful Aphrodite was procreated in the foam of the waves.
>
> (Allende 1998, 137)

Since the late 1990s, the tendency towards using Aphrodite's name as a cover inducement has been followed by several other authors and publishers. The target audience for this unique marketing, however, is not always easy to categorize or even discern, as Aphrodite's name is used in numerous topic areas and disciplines. Yet the essential goal is always evident: these book titles aim to evoke the concepts of beauty, love and sexuality signified by the Greek goddess. Although it might be expected that the name "Aphrodite" would be utilized for collections of literary erotica, that is, poems and short fiction on sexual themes, lately the name is more commonly used in non-fiction works describing personal experiences of sexual learning or awakening. Two recent examples are Jalaja Bonheim's *Aphrodite's Daughters: Women's Sexual Stories and the Journey of the Soul* (1997) and Jeanette Jaffe-Longoria's *Aphrodite and Me:*

Discovering Sensuality and Romance At Any Age (2004). An astonishing collection of female nude photographs by Terry Lorant, with text by Dr. Loren Eskenazi, *Reconstructing Aphrodite* (2001), documents the physical transformation of twenty-one breast cancer survivors after reconstructive surgery, emphasizing the enduring beauty and strength of the women's bodies. Aphrodite also appears in the category of bedroom décor, as in Elisabeth Millar's *Releasing Aphrodite: Aromatic Aphrodisiacs for Love and Romance* (2006), a guide to using fragrance to enhance erotic enjoyment. In romance novels, Aphrodite's name is used for the most obvious effect in luring customers, for example in Stuart Harrison's *Aphrodite's Smile: A Mesmerizing Novel of Passion and Suspense* (2004), which hardly seems to need its self-congratulatory subtitle. Romance author Julie Kenner's mass market Aphrodite Series includes *Aphrodite's Kiss* (2001), *Aphrodite's Passion* (2002), *Aphrodite's Secret* (2003) and *Aphrodite's Flame* (2004). And in a return to the goddess' own literary roots in ancient Greek verse, poet Becky Gould Gibson's latest volume of poetry is entitled *Aphrodite's Daughter* (2008). Even this modest selection of examples from the field of publishing reveals the high promotional value and impact in making use of the brand name Aphrodite.

Perhaps the ancient Greek epigrammatist, Antipater of Thessalonica (*ca.* first century BC), was rather prophetic in recognizing the entrepreneurial implications of marketing the name and image of Aphrodite. According to Antipater, the goddess is just like Nestor, the legendary king of ancient Pylos, who ruled over three generations of mortals (*Iliad* 1.250–52), since Aphrodite currently controls all three human cohorts of the most costly and precious metals. In these amusing verses, the poet seems to imply that love and money go hand in (open) hand.

> There was a golden age, and a bronze and a silver
> back in the day, but nowadays Cytherea is all three in one.
> She honors the golden man and loves the bronze man
> and never turns away from the silver ones.
> The Paphian is practically like Nestor!
> I even think that Zeus, when he came to Danaë,
> was not himself gold, but the bearer of a hundred gold coins.
>
> (*Greek Anthology* 5.31, author's translation)

FILM AND TELEVISION

The goddess Aphrodite has also made her debut on the silver screen, both big and small. In recent years, there has been a resurgence of film and television productions that depict the ancient Greek and Roman worlds, with filmmakers and television producers using several different classical sources for their creative inspiration. Some screen recreations are set directly in Greco-Roman antiquity, while other films and television programs utilize classical mythological and literary plots, themes and archetypes. Aphrodite's on-screen appearances have occurred in both categories, as each type of production serves to highlight the visual potential of portraying her most important physical characteristics as well as her many accompanying stories and attributes. While the image of the Roman Venus continues to occur more often in cinematic references to the ancient goddess of love, sex and beauty, Aphrodite enjoys a few noteworthy appearances in modern films and television productions, as the following brief survey will demonstrate.

During the heyday of the big-screen epic cinema in the 1950s and early 1960s, a subcategory of Italian sword-and-sandal films known as the "*peplum* films" became immensely popular and commercially profitable. Set in antiquity, many of these films derived their plots, often quite loosely, from Greco-Roman history or mythology. In 1958, two films featuring the name and image of Aphrodite were produced, where both films also utilized the visual and narrative motif of statues of the goddess (for brief summaries of these two films: Elley 1984). The first film, *Aphrodite, Goddess of Love* (1958), originally released under the title *La Venere di Cheronea* (1958), was a joint Italian and French production directed by Fernando Cerchio and Victor Tourjansky, and starring Belinda Lee and Massimo Girotti. The story takes place during Greece's war with Macedonia, just before the battle of Chaeronea in 338 BC, and focuses on the historical sculptor Praxiteles (Girotti) and the beautiful servant Iris (Lee), his model for the famed Aphrodite of Knidos. One day Iris finds an injured Macedonian soldier, Lucian (Jacques Sernas), washed up on the beach, and so naturally the two fall in love. When Praxiteles becomes jealous of their happiness, he betrays Lucian to the Greek army. In despair, Iris runs away from the sculptor to try to find her lover, but she is soon captured by the Greek soldiers. After Lucian escapes, he rescues Iris and the two are blissfully reunited at the end of the film. But the true cinematic climax is the scene in Praxiteles' studio where the artist fends off the Macedonian soldiers from his famous statue of Aphrodite.

In the same year, Mario Bonnard directed *Afrodite, dea dell'amore* (1958), also known by its English title *Slave Women of Corinth* (1958), starring Isabelle Corey and Antonio de Teffè. This film likewise centers on an artist as protagonist who is faced with a romantic dilemma. In Corinth in the year AD 67, the local governor, Antigonus (Ivo Garrani), wishes to curry favor with the Roman emperor, Nero. So he commissions a renowned sculptor, Demetrius (de Teffè), to create a new statue of the goddess Aphrodite for the city's temple. Now Demetrius is forced to choose between two female models: Diala (Irène Tunc), the ambitious Phoenician courtesan who seduced Antigonus, and Lerna (Corey), the kind and gentle blonde slave girl, who is also a fervent Christian. According to the generic conventions of such films, Demetrius falls in love with Lerna and converts to the new faith. After much action and intrigue, the local Christians are all arrested and sentenced to death, and Demetrius and Lerna are only saved by the timely intervention of the Roman army, who restore order to the chaotic city of Corinth. Thus, both of these *peplum* films employ, with varying levels of success, the theme of the Greek artist's romantic love for a beautiful female model against the narrative and visual backdrop of his creation of a statue of Aphrodite, goddess of beauty and erotic desire.

The statue of Aphrodite as a cinematic motif is also twice replayed in visual impressions in two very different films (on the use of mythological allusions as visual cinematic quotations: Solomon 2001). In director Stanley Kubrick's *Spartacus* (1960), a scene takes place in the villa of the populist patrician Roman senator Gracchus (Charles Laughton). In the middle background of the scene, just behind the dinner table loaded with gourmet delicacies, the set decorator has placed a copy of the Knidian Aphrodite. The conspicuous presence of the statue in this scene accentuates the cultural refinement of the wealthy and elite Senator Gracchus, while at the same time drawing his character as a rather louche and hedonistic man who loves women. "I have a promiscuous nature," Gracchus admits in this scene. "And, unlike these aristocrats, I will not take a marriage vow . . . which I know my nature will prevent me from keeping." The senator's taste in art as portrayed in his villa confirms his disposition as much as the lines of dialogue from the screenplay do.

In a much later film, the Knidia type appears again, this time in the macabre comedy *Death Becomes Her* (1992), directed by Robert Zemeckis. The film stars Meryl Streep and Goldie Hawn as two rival *femmes fatales* seeking to attain eternal youth and beauty. In a crucial scene, the undead Madeline (Streep) furiously confronts Helen (Hawn) on her opulent patio, which is classically decorated with a large pool of water and a marble copy of the Knidian Aphrodite set in a wall niche. Madeline takes a shotgun and blasts a dinner-plate size hole in her rival's abdomen, and as the Aphrodite statue looks on, Helen falls backwards into the pool. But Helen has also drunk the magic rejuvenation elixir, so she can't die – rather, as she emerges from the water like the sea-born goddess herself, the camera focuses on the hole in her stomach, through which the Knidia can clearly be seen. "Just look at me," shrieks Helen. "I'm all wet!" In this darkly comic scene, the presence of Aphrodite's statue helps to define the fundamental theme of the film, that is, the women's extreme lust for youth, beauty and immortality.

Aphrodite appears as an actual divine character in the celebrated mythological film *Clash of the Titans* (1981), directed by Desmond Davis and produced by famed special effects creator, Ray Harryhausen. The film is based rather freely on the myth of the Greek hero Perseus (Harry Hamlin), who performs various feats of strength and daring, as the Olympian gods look on from above and manipulate his fate with divine petulance. An all-star cast of celebrity thespians fill the roles of the meddlesome Greek deities, including Laurence Olivier as Zeus, Claire Bloom as Hera, and Maggie Smith as Thetis. In the role of Aphrodite, who helps Perseus pursue his romance with the princess Andromeda (Judi Bowker), the filmmakers cast stunning Swiss beauty Ursula Andress. Nearly twenty years earlier, Andress was featured in one of the most famous sequences in all of film history: this is the scene in *Dr. No* (1962), the first official James Bond film, where shell diver Honey Ryder (Andress) emerges from the ocean, like the newly born Aphrodite herself, wearing the now-legendary white bikini. As a visual trope for introducing a beautiful and sexually powerful female character, the scene has become so iconic that it has been repeatedly referenced in several other films over the past five decades, including recently by actress Halle Berry as Bond girl Jinx in the film *Die Another Day* (2002). Thus, the bikini scene would have had the effect of reinforcing Andress' identification with the sea-born goddess Aphrodite in *Clash of the Titans*, as the movie audience would certainly be aware of her nearly mythical emergence from the waves of Dr. No's Caribbean island in the earlier film. An extra-cinematic association between the actress and the Greek goddess of love was also at work during the filming of *Clash of the Titans*, as Andress became romantically involved with her much younger heroic co-star Hamlin, and gave birth to a son, Dimitri, her only child, at the end of the shoot. So after being cast as the perfect Aphrodite, Andress seemed to live the part.

Although not actually set in Greco-Roman antiquity, several other modern films refer to or evoke the name, image and mythical narratives of Aphrodite. For example, *The Adventures of Baron Munchausen* (1989), a fantastical action film directed by Terry Gilliam of Monty Python fame, contains a striking mythological sequence that showcases the familiar motif of the goddess' marine birth. During one of his adventures, the Baron (John Neville) finds himself at the home of the god Vulcan (Oliver Reed) when a huge bivalve seashell mechanically opens up to reveal the lovely blonde goddess (Uma Thurman) inside, who is

Figure 7.1 Aphrodite (Ursula Andress) in *Clash of the Titans* (1981). MGM/The Kobal Collection.

standing completely naked in the pose of the Knidian Aphrodite. Two lithe, brunette handmaidens fly gracefully towards her carrying long white swathes of diaphanous cloth, which they drape around her in wide, airborne circles until she is fully clothed. The scene is a clear visual homage to Sandro Botticelli's celebrated painting *The Birth of Venus* (ca. 1485), which in turn was inspired by the famous ancient nude statue sculpted by Praxiteles. In contemporary cinema, Aphrodite's *anodos*

Figure 7.2 Honey Ryder (Ursula Andress) in *Dr. No* (1962). DANJAQ/EON/UA/The Kobal Collection.

from the sea remains one of the most potent and distinctive emblems of her divinity.

Director Woody Allen's comedy film *Mighty Aphrodite* (1995) only uses the name of the goddess in the title, but its plot is based on the ancient myth of Pygmalion, a sculptor from the island of Cyprus who fell in love with a statue he created. Like the two Aphrodite-titled *peplum* films from the 1950s, *Mighty Aphrodite* explores the theme of the male subjective aspiration or need to fashion the female form and consciousness: in this film, sports writer Lenny (Allen) seeks to reshape the lifestyle of the genial prostitute Linda (Mira Sorvino). In addition to the mythological background, *Mighty Aphrodite* has the dramatic trappings of an ancient Greek play, including several literary characters who drop in on the action (such as Jocasta, Oedipus and Teiresias), as well as a Greek chorus commenting on the story, whose scenes were filmed at the Teatro Greco in Taormina on the island of Sicily. While the film's title imbues it with a classical ambience, the alluring name of the goddess suggests its artistic and romantic themes.

The musical *Mamma Mia!* (2008), directed by Phyllida Lloyd and starring Meryl Streep and Pierce Brosnan, takes place on a small Greek island called Kalokairi "Summertime" in the film (shot on location on the Greek island of Skopelos), where feisty single mother Donna (Streep) runs a shabby villa hotel that is said to occupy the ancient site of Aphrodite's sacred fountain. Amid much raucous dancing and singing, the plot revolves around Donna's daughter, young bride-to-be Sophie (Amanda Seyfried), who, unbeknownst to her Mom, wishes to discover the identity of her father, who turns out to be handsome, successful architect Sam (Brosnan). At the end of the film, when the parental couple are reunited and everyone else is paired off in romantic duos, and as the wedding party is in full swing, a tremor splits open the dolphin mosaic in the center of the dance floor, and a tall spray of water gushes out and rains over all the revelers. In the midst of the refreshing shower, Donna cries out, "It's Aphrodite!" as she realizes the true source of this divine intervention, inspiring everyone to find love and get soaking wet at the same time.

In the realm of television, Aphrodite has appeared as a character on two important and influential series that employ ancient mythological motifs and narratives. First came *Hercules: The Legendary Journeys* (1995–1999), starring Kevin Sorbo in the title role, which was based very loosely on the tales of the Greek hero Heracles, and eventually became the most popular syndicated television series in the world. *Hercules'* success inspired several other television programs set in antiquity, including a wildly popular spin-off and major cult favorite *Xena: Warrior Princess* (1995–2001), starring Lucy Lawless as the titular heroine. Both series are historical fantasies set primarily in ancient Greece, yet they are built around a flexible mix of timelines, settings and events where various mythological and historical characters appear together and interact freely: this medley approach seemed only to heighten the two series' quirky appeal to fans. On both series, the goddess Aphrodite (Alexandra Tydings) appears in numerous episodes as a significant character, the goddess of love. Aphrodite is portrayed as a cute, curvaceous young woman with long curly blonde hair, who exudes the fresh-faced allure of the "California beach girl," and she is typically dressed in skimpy lingerie or bikini outfits that are often translucent, rosy pink and frothy. As a character, she is generally portrayed as cheerful, fun-loving and helpful to humans, but sometimes devious and scheming, and a few of her story-lines display her petty and even vengeful nature. Aphrodite first appears on the series *Hercules* (in "The Apple," Season 2, Episode 17), when a large scallop shell is shown floating towards the beach. The shell opens up to reveal Aphrodite inside, who stretches and yawns as if just waking from sleep; she then stands up and uses the shell as a windsurf board to sail into shore, turning the canonical "birth from the sea" motif into an amusing tableau. On the series *Xena*, Aphrodite eventually develops a close sisterly bond with Gabrielle (Renée O'Connor), Xena's intimate companion, and for this reason the goddess remains neutral during the final deadly conflict between Xena and the Olympians (in "Mother-hood," Season 5, Episode 22). The narrative of the show implies that after the climactic "Twilight of the Gods," Aphrodite is one of only two Greek gods, along with Ares, to survive into the modern day.

On the short-lived romantic comedy series *Valentine* (2008–2009), Aphrodite appeared as the main protagonist. The show's premise is that a family of ancient Greek gods has come down to earth to live in modern-day Los Angeles, where they have assumed contemporary identities as they work to bring erotic soulmates together. At the head of the family business is matriarch Grace Valentine (Jaime Murray), who is actually the goddess Aphrodite: against customary physical type, Aphrodite is portrayed as a sleek, elegant brunette with a posh accent and an ironic smirk. She is married to the powerful, smug war contractor Ari, the god Ares (Greg Ellis), but she has an ongoing love affair with her ex-husband, affable handyman Ray Howard, the god Hephaestus (Patrick Fabian). Grace tries to control her unruly son Danny Valentine, the god Eros (Kristoffer Polaha), who spends his time out partying and seducing women, as he wields a dangerous love gun that shoots desire at his unsuspecting targets. Regrettably, the series only aired for four ori-ginal episodes in the fall of 2008, while the remaining four unaired epi-sodes were "burned off" in the summer of 2009. Although the quality of the writing tended to be rather uneven, the series *Valentine* exhibited in its brief lifespan an unique potential to showcase a more progressive and modern Aphrodite, one who channeled her divine influence over the realm of love and sexuality into an activist enterprise both profitable and benevolent.

OVERVIEW

In our inquiry into Aphrodite's career after Greek antiquity, we see that the goddess' authority as an emblem of beauty, adornment, love and sexuality remains undiminished. After Rome emerged on the ancient scene, we noted how the overlapping figures of Greek Aphrodite and Roman Venus influenced each other, as Aphrodite's character became more maternal, martial and administrative during later Greek antiquity. Yet while Roman Venus dominated the canonical genres of Western art and literature throughout the following centuries, the name and image of Aphrodite is experiencing a rebirth in the present-day popular awareness, so that Aphrodite's commercial value as a brand name is now genuinely appreciated. In contemporary beauty marketing, fashion advertising and book publishing, the name and image of "Aphrodite" are successfully employed to attract customers, capitalizing on the goddess' familiar symbolic connection to the enhancement of physical beauty for the purpose of erotic allure. Likewise, Aphrodite's appearances in modern films and television programs highlight her marine origins, her celebrated artistic incarnation as the Knidia, and her compelling and continuing sway over the realms of love and beauty. Today, more than ever, Aphrodite is an enduring and eloquent symbol of the feminine divine.

FURTHER READING

The following list includes works cited in the preceding chapters as well as items of interest for further reading.

MAJOR PRIMARY SOURCES

Homer, *Iliad*, trans. Stanley Lombardo (1997), *Homer: Iliad*. Indianapolis: Hackett.

Homer, *Odyssey*, trans. Stanley Lombardo (2000), *Homer: Odyssey*. Indianapolis: Hackett.

Hesiod, *Theogony* and *Works and Days*, trans. Stanley Lombardo (1993), *Hesiod: Works and Days, Theogony*. Indianapolis: Hackett.

The Homeric Hymns, trans. Sarah Ruden (2005), *Homeric Hymns*. Indianapolis: Hackett.

Hesiod, Homeric Hymns, Epic Cycle, Homerica, trans. Hugh G. Evelyn-White (1936), Loeb Classical Library: new and revised edition. Cambridge and London: Harvard University Press.

The Greek Lyric Poets, trans. Andrew M. Miller (1996), *Greek Lyric: An Anthology in Translation*. Indianapolis: Hackett.

Herodotus, *The Histories*, trans. Henry Cary (1992), *The History: Herodotus*. Buffalo: Prometheus Books.

Euripides, *Hippolytus*, trans. Diane Arnson Svarlien (2007), *Euripides: Alcestis, Medea, Hippolytus*. Indianapolis: Hackett.

The Greek Anthology, trans. Kenneth Rexroth (1999), *Poems from the Greek Anthology*, 2nd edition. Ann Arbor: University of Michigan Press.

Apollonius Rhodius, *Argonautica*, trans. Richard Hunter (1993), *Apollonius of Rhodes: Jason and the Golden Fleece*. Oxford: Oxford University Press.

Bion, *Lament for Adonis*, trans. J.D. Reed (1997), *Bion of Smyrna: The Fragments and the Adonis*. Cambridge: Cambridge University Press.

Vergil, *Aeneid*, trans. Stanley Lombardo (2005), *Vergil: Aeneid*. Indianapolis: Hackett.

SECONDARY SOURCES

Aphrodite in art, literature and culture

Allende, Isabel (1998). *Aphrodite: A Memoir of the Senses*. New York: HarperCollins.

Barrett, W. S., ed. (1964). *Euripides: Hippolytos*. Oxford: Oxford University Press.

Bergren, Ann (1989). *"The Homeric Hymn to Aphrodite*: Tradition and Rhetoric, Praise and Blame." *Classical Antiquity* 8: 1–41.

Bittrich, Ursula (2005). *Aphrodite und Eros in der antiken Tragödie: Mit Ausblicken auf motivgeschichtlich verwandte Dichtungen.* Berlin and New York: Walter de Gruyter.

Boedeker, Deborah Dickmann (1974). *Aphrodite's Entry into Greek Epic*. Leiden: E.J. Brill.

Böhm, Stephanie (1990). *Die "Nackte Göttin": zur Ikonographie und Deutung unbekleideter weiblicher Figuren in der frühgriechischen Kunst.* Mainz: Verlag Philipp von Zabern.

Bolger, Diane and Serwint, Nancy, eds. (2002). *Engendering Aphrodite: Women and Society in Ancient Cyprus*. Boston: ASOR (American Schools of Oriental Research).

Breitenberger, Barbara (2007). *Aphrodite and Eros: The Development of Erotic Mythology in Early Greek Poetry and Culture*. New York and London: Routledge.

Budin, Stephanie Lynn (2003). *The Origin of Aphrodite*. Bethesda: CDL Press.

—— (2009). "Aphrodite Enoplion." In *Brill's Companion to Aphrodite*, eds. Amy C. Smith and Sadie Pickup. Leiden: E.J. Brill.

Caldwell, Richard S., ed. (1987). *Hesiod's Theogony*. Newburyport, MA: Focus Publishing.

Clay, Jenny Strauss (1989). *The Politics of Olympus: Form and Meaning in the Major Homeric Hymns*. Princeton: Princeton University Press.

Cyrino, Monica (1993). "Shame, Danger and Desire: Aphrodite's Power in the Fifth Homeric Hymn." *Rocky Mountain Review of Language and Literature* 47.4: 219–30.

Detienne, Marcel (1972). *Les Jardins d'Adonis*. Paris: Gallimard. Trans. by Janet Lloyd (1994). *The Gardens of Adonis: Spices in Greek Mythology*. 2nd edition. Princeton: Princeton University Press.

Elley, Derek (1984). *The Epic Film: Myth and History*. London: Routledge and Kegan Paul.

Faulkner, Andrew (2008). *The Homeric Hymn to Aphrodite: Introduction, Text, and Commentary*. Oxford: Oxford University Press.

Flemberg, Johan (1991). *Venus Armata: Studien zur bewaffneten Aphrodite in der griechisch-römischen Kunst*. Stockholm: Paul Aströms Förlag.

Friedrich, Paul (1978). *The Meaning of Aphrodite*. Chicago: University of Chicago Press.

Goff, Barbara E. (1990). *The Noose of Words: Readings of Desire, Violence and Language in Euripides'* Hippolytos. Cambridge: Cambridge University Press.

Greene, Ellen, ed. (1996). *Reading Sappho: Contemporary Approaches*. Berkeley and Los Angeles: University of California Press.

Grigson, Geoffrey (1976). *The Goddess of Love: The Birth, Triumph, Death and Return of Aphrodite*. London: Constable.

Gutzwiller, Kathryn J. (1998). *Poetic Garlands: Hellenistic Epigrams in Context*. Berkeley and Los Angeles: University of California Press.

Havelock, Christine Mitchell (1995). *The Aphrodite of Knidos and her Successors: A Historical Review of the Female Nude in Greek Art*. Ann Arbor: University of Michigan Press.

Heimpel, Wolfgang (1982). "A Catalog of Near Eastern Venus Deities." *Syro-Mesopotamian Studies* 4.3: 9–22.

Hunter, R.L., ed. (1989). *Apollonius of Rhodes: Argonautica Book III*. Cambridge: Cambridge University Press.

Johnson, Buffie (1994). *Lady of the Beasts: The Goddess and her Sacred Animals*. Rochester, Vermont: Inner Traditions International.

Karageorghis, Jacqueline (2005). *Kypris: The Aphrodite of Cyprus: Ancient Sources and Archaeological Evidence*. Nicosia: A.G. Leventis Foundation.

Larson, Jennifer (2001). *Greek Nymphs: Myth, Cult, Lore*. Oxford and New York: Oxford University Press.

—— (2007). *Ancient Greek Cults: A Guide*. London and New York: Routledge.

MacLachlan, Bonnie (1993). *The Age of Grace: Charis in Early Greek Poetry*. Princeton: Princeton University Press.

Mills, Sophie (2002). *Euripides: Hippolytus*. London: Duckworth.

Moorey, P. R. S. (2004). *Idols of the People: Miniature Images of Clay in the Ancient Near East*. Oxford: Oxford University Press.

Nagy, Gregory (1990). *Greek Mythology and Poetics*. Ithaca: Cornell University Press.

—— (1996). *Homeric Questions*. Austin: University of Texas Press.

Pirenne-Delforge, Vinciane (1994). *L' Aphrodite grecque: Contribution à l' étude de ses cultes et de sa personnalité dans le panthéon archaïque et classique. Kernos Supplément* 4. Athens and Liège: Centre International d'Étude de la Religion Grecque Antique.

—— (2007). " 'Something to do with Aphrodite': *Ta Aphrodisia* and the Sacred." In *A Companion to Greek Religion*, ed. Daniel Ogden. Malden and Oxford: Blackwell Publishing. 311–23.

Pironti, Gabriella (2007). *Entre ciel et guerre: Figures d' Aphrodite en Grèce ancienne. Kernos Supplément* 18. Athens and Liège: Centre International d'Étude de la Religion Grecque Antique.

Podbielski, Henryk (1971). *La Structure de l' Hymne Homérique à Aphrodite à la lumière de la tradition littéraire*. Wroclaw: Polska Akademia Nauk.

Rayor, Diane J. (2004). *The Homeric Hymns*. Berkeley and Los Angeles: University of California Press.

Rosenzweig, Rachel (2004). *Worshipping Aphrodite: Art and Cult in Classical Athens*. Ann Arbor: University of Michigan Press.

Rudhardt, Jean (1986). *Le role d'Eros et d'Aphrodite dans les cosmogonies grecques*. Paris: Presses Universitaires de France.

Schilling, Robert (1982). *La religion romaine de Vénus, depuis les origins jusqu'au temps d'Auguste.* 2nd edition. Paris: E. de Boccard.

Smith, Amy C. and Pickup, Sadie, eds. (2009). *Brill's Companion to Aphrodite.* Leiden: E.J. Brill.

Smith, Peter (1981). *Nursling of Mortality: A Study of the Homeric Hymn to Aphrodite. Studien zur klassischen Philologie* 3. Frankfurt: Peter Lang.

Solomon, Jon (2001). *The Ancient World in the Cinema.* Revised and expanded edition. New Haven and London: Yale University Press.

Ulbrich, Anja (2008). *Kypris: Heiligtümer und Kulte weiblicher Gottheiten auf Zypern in der kyproarchaischen und kyproklassiischen Epoche (Königszeit).* Münster: Ugarit-Verlag.

van Eck, Johannes (1978). *The Homeric Hymn to Aphrodite: Introduction, Commentary and Appendices.* Ph.D. dissertation, Utrecht University.

Wallensten, Jennifer (2009). "Aphrodite between Greece and Rome: Greek Responses to the Idea of Aphrodite as Ancestress of the Romans." In *Brill's Companion to Aphrodite,* eds. Amy C. Smith and Sadie Pickup. Leiden: E.J. Brill.

West, M.L. (1997). *The East Face of Helicon.* Oxford: Oxford University Press.

—— (2000). "The Name of Aphrodite." *Glotta* 76: 133–38.

Love and sexuality in the ancient world

Budin, Stephanie Lynn (2008). *The Myth of Sacred Prostitution in Antiquity.* Cambridge: Cambridge University Press.

Calame, Claude (1999). *The Poetics of Eros in Ancient Greece.* Trans. Janet Lloyd. Princeton: Princeton University Press.

Carson, Anne (1986). *Eros the Bittersweet.* Princeton: Princeton University Press.

Cyrino, Monica S. (1995). *In Pandora's Jar: Lovesickness in Early Greek Poetry.* Lanham: University Press of America.

Davidson, James (1997). *Courtesans and Fishcakes: The Consuming Passions of Classical Athens.* New York: HarperCollins.

Faraone, Christopher A. (1999). *Ancient Greek Love Magic.* Cambridge: Harvard University Press.

Faraone, Christopher A. and McClure, Laura K., eds. (2006). *Prostitutes and Courtesans in the Ancient World.* Madison: University of Wisconsin Press.

Garrison, Daniel H. (2000). *Sexual Culture in Ancient Greece.* Norman: University of Oklahoma Press.

Golden, Mark and Toohey, Peter, eds. (2003). *Sex and Difference in Ancient Greece and Rome.* Edinburgh: Edinburgh University Press.

Halperin, David M., Winkler, John J., and Zeitlin, Froma I., eds. (1990). *Before Sexuality: The Construction of Erotic Experience in the Ancient Greek World.* Princeton: Princeton University Press.

Henry, Madeleine M. (1995). *Prisoner of History: Aspasia of Miletus and Her Biographical Tradition.* Oxford: Oxford University Press.

Johnson, Marguerite and Ryan, Terry (2005). *Sexuality in Greek and Roman Society and Literature: A Sourcebook.* London and New York: Routledge.

Kampen, Natalie Boymel, ed. (1996). *Sexuality in Ancient Art.* Cambridge: Cambridge University Press.

McClure, Laura K., ed. (2002). *Sexuality and Gender in the Classical World: Readings and Sources.* Malden and Oxford: Blackwell Publishing.

McClure, Laura K. (2003). *Courtesans at Table: Gender and Greek Literary Culture in Athenaeus.* New York and London: Routledge.

Nussbaum, Martha C. and Sihvola, Juha, eds. (2002). *The Sleep of Reason: Erotic Experience and Sexual Ethics in Ancient Greece and Rome.* Chicago: University of Chicago Press.

Richlin, Amy, ed. (1992). *Pornography and Representation in Greece and Rome.* Oxford: Oxford University Press.

Sissa, Giulia (2008). *Sex and Sensuality in the Ancient World.* Trans. George Staunton. New Haven and London: Yale University Press.

Skinner, Marilyn B. (2005). *Sexuality in Greek and Roman Culture.* Malden and Oxford: Blackwell Publishing.

Stewart, Andrew (1997). *Art, Desire, and the Body in Ancient Greece.* Cambridge: Cambridge University Press.

Thornton, Bruce S. (1997). *Eros: The Myth of Ancient Greek Sexuality.* Boulder: Westview Press.

Winkler, John J. (1990). *The Constraints of Desire: The Anthropology of Sex and Gender in Ancient Greece.* New York and London: Routledge.

Wohl, Victoria (2002). *Love Among the Ruins: The Erotics of Democracy in Classical Athens.* Princeton: Princeton University Press.

Zeitlin, Froma I. (1996). *Playing the Other: Gender and Society in Classical Greek Literature.* Chicago: University of Chicago Press.

INDEX